Skelton Revealed

SKELTON REVEALED

Eleven centuries of history and heritage

Editor: Peter Appleton

BgB

Boroughgate Books

Published by Boroughgate Books

ISBN 978-0-9933674-3-4

Book layout and cover design by:
Boroughgate Books

Website: www.boroughgate-books.co.uk

Skelton Townscape Heritage Project was made possible by the following organisations:

Dedicated to the memory of Tony Harding

Contents

Preface

This book marks the culmination of Skelton History Group's involvement with the Townscape Heritage project, which ran from 2015 into 2021, and which was National Lottery Heritage Fund-supported. Throughout that time, our knowledge and research expertise were called upon regularly. As Secretary of the group, and a Skelton born and bred individual, my personal memories and accumulated knowledge were called upon time and time again. But by far the most onerous, and yet most enjoyable, task was the production of this book.

It would never have come about were it not for the authors of the articles. As editor, I give you all my earnest thanks. You have done a magnificent job. Your passion for your subject shines through. I have tried to preserve your words, restricting my editorial actions wherever possible to standardising the use of fonts across all the articles. I hope you feel I have succeeded.

Publication of this book will, hopefully, generate a small but steady income to Skelton Villages Civic Pride. This income will be used, in the first place, to pay the on-going costs associated with keeping the project's website active after the end of the project. Any surplus will be added to that group's general funds. The project's website can be found here:

skeltontownscapeheritage.org.uk

Finally, I hope that reading this book will give as much pleasure to you, now reading it, as researching, writing, and producing it has to the authors and myself.

Peter Appleton
Skelton Green
December 2020

Introduction

Brenda Harding

Residents and visitors alike are enjoying the transformation of Skelton-in-Cleveland's High Street. New shop fronts, evoking the village's heritage, are surrounded by new pavements, benches, trees and tubs and baskets of flowers, a series of mosaics adorn the walls of shops and houses. Many of these changes have been driven by Skelton Villages Civic Pride (SVCP). Other groups, inspired by the successes of SVCP activities, have had more specific objectives. For example, the Friends of Skelton Community Orchard (FOSCO) turned abandoned allotment land into a beautiful community orchard and park. They also were the driving force behind the magnificent sculpture of three ironstone miners which stands proudly near Cross Green.

The largest of all these projects was the one that sought to transform the appearance of the High Street. Part of the funding for this was provided by the National Lottery's Heritage Fund for the development of Townscape Heritage Schemes. To understand how the project began we need to go back to November 2011 when SVCP was established as a voluntary group holding weekly coffee mornings at Skelton Civic Hall. It aimed to bring together the people of the four villages of Skelton, thus helping to avoid social isolation, at the same time raising funds towards improving the local environment. [The four villages are: Skelton-in-Cleveland, Skelton Green, North Skelton, and New Skelton. Ed.]

When they heard that Heritage Lottery grants were available, Joyce White and Pam Batts, both members of SVCP, had the idea of getting one of these grants for Skelton. So, in January 2013, Joyce and her husband Stuart, conducted a survey of all the occupiers of properties on the High Street, to ascertain the level of support for the scheme. Lengthy discussions were held with 24 local retailers who were told that Heritage money could be available to enable them to have their shop fronts replaced with a more traditional design, in keeping with the history of the village. As a result of this research, Pam Batts and Joyce White considered they had a viable proposal which they presented to the SVCP Committee on 28th January 2013.

The Committee agreed to go ahead with an application and employed a Consultant to assist with the paperwork for the first round of the application. This first application to the National Lottery was rejected but, undeterred, SVCP tried again, submitting a revised application in August 2014. Now working in partnership with Redcar and Cleveland Borough Council, Tees Valley Rural Community Council [later to become Tees Valley Rural Action], Skelton and Gilling Estates, and Skelton History Group, their plan was to restore the heritage of Skelton, and to raise the public's awareness of the rich history of the area, SVCP's key proposals were:

- Replace unsympathetic shop fronts with facades that evoked the early 20th C through their design, including reinstated architectural details.
- Improve and upgrade the built fabric of the High Street, replacing pavements, adding new seating and parking facilities, and planting trees and flower beds.
- Erect a mosaic illustrating the history of the development of the village, and a mosaic trail highlighting 19th and early 20th C village trades and activities. These would be designed by local groups and schools and developed by two local mosaic artists.
- Hold further community activities and events once the scheme was underway.
- Capture memories through recorded and transcribed interviews with older residents.
- Document the buildings within the conservation area by written description, drawing and photography,

providing a "baseline" of the village that future generations could refer to.

- Investigate the archaeology of Boroughgate Field, the presumed site of early medieval Skelton, through a programme of work led by Robin Daniels of Tees Archaeology, and assisted by Skelton History Group, local volunteers, school children, and college students.

To everyone's relief, in February 2015 the National Lottery Heritage Fund announced that the grant application from Skelton had been successful.

A Management Board was set up, office premises in the High Street were found, and John Haw, a retired Town Planner, Surveyor and Urban Regeneration Consultant, was appointed as Project Manager. Initially working from home, he moved into the new office at 97 High Street on 20th July 2015 and from then on it was all systems go.

A further funding bid had to be submitted and plans drawn up showing how all the projects would be managed. John was at first assisted by Joyce White, but when ill-health forced her resignation, her place was taken by Tony Harding, a retired NHS professional. This second bid was successful and on 16th June 2016 the Heritage Lottery Grant scheme awarded Skelton Townscape Heritage Project £952,000. With 'match-funding' from Redcar and Cleveland Borough Council, Skelton and Brotton Parish Council, Skelton and Gilling Estate and SVCP, the final amount raised was £1.4 million, and work began on the High Street's regeneration in 2017.

The work of the community groups has continued. SVCP's fund-raising coffee mornings raise money that helps to pay for the numerous tubs and hanging baskets which adorn the High Street. Inspired by the changes being brought about in the village, the magnificent sculpture of three working miners, entitled *"The Spirit of East Cleveland"*, was made by Bill Harland, a Skelton resident who also happens to be sculptor by profession. The money to pay for this was raised by FOSCO. Their team of volunteer gardeners have continued to develop the wonderful Ringrose Orchard, built entirely by their volunteer effort. This provides an attractive introduction to Skelton for walkers using the Cleveland Way National Trail as it passes through the village.

Read on to learn more about what was done, and what was learned, during the Townscape Heritage project. But, as you read, remember that much of what happened was through the involvement of volunteers, who freely gave their time and expertise to their village because they were proud of it.

[During the life of the Townscape Heritage project, the effort provided by the volunteers raised a cash-equivalent contribution of more than £220,000. This was two-thirds more than expected! Ed.]

Shopping in Victorian Skelton

Josie Bland and Eugenie Noonan

Skelton is discovering its heritage. Many of the High Street shops, from the Post Office to the Amber Rooms, and Hair Expressions opposite, have had their frontages refurbished in the style of the early 1900s. This has been funded with support from the National Lottery, and from the shop owners themselves. Here, we look in detail at the way this part of the High Street changed in the latter half of the nineteenth century, discuss the shoppers' lives and their shopping habits, and focus on three of the shops involved in the refurbishment, and the families who lived in them.

Nowadays the availability of cars and refrigeration has resulted in the development of large supermarkets and out-of-town shopping. We shop by car and drive home with laden bags. Skelton High Street has become a place of leisure, where the beauty industry mingles with micro bars, a Tea Shop and Delicatessen, and where the Co-op, now a 'convenience store', sells hummus, falafel and goat's cheese. But what would we find if we turn back the clock?

Map of Skelton 1850s (detail).

From the 1860s onwards, the small, rural village of Skelton in Cleveland, with its community of farmers and tradespeople, was overwhelmed by an onslaught of newcomers from all corners of Britain, after a seam of ironstone had been discovered in the Cleveland Hills. As new ironstone mines opened around Skelton, the first in 1861, men came looking for work, many with their families in tow. Wave after wave of coal miners from West Yorkshire, Durham, Northumberland and Scotland, agricultural workers from Norfolk and Lincolnshire, and tin miners from Cornwall arrived to swell the work force. The population in 1861 for Skelton, North Skelton, Lingdale and Boosbeck comprised 517 males and 517 females. By 1871 the numbers had more than doubled – 1490 males and 1071 females - and had quadrupled by 1881 – 4224 males and 3596 females. Houses had to be built for them and shops opened.

As the village grew, so did the High Street. The map (previous page) shows that, in the 1850s, the now refurbished section of the High Street was unbuilt apart from two farms, West Rossa and East Rossa.

Skelton from the Hills. 1876 approx.

By 1876, the houses and shops from 79 to 129 had been built. The Wharton Arms, previously standing on the site of the present-day Fire Station, was built in 1878 and All Saints parish church was consecrated in 1884. By 1881 we had a recognisable High Street, although most of the opposite side, which had been a sandstone quarry, and later was given over to allotments, was unbuilt. The population continued to expand. Let us look at the shops that served this stretch of the High Street in 1881.

William Young, 57, had a butcher's shop at 121, which is now Joe Coral's Bookmakers. A shoemaker, or cordwainer, William Knaggs, was at 97-99, and another shoemaker, John Cornforth was in residence at number 115, now Mrs Blairs. Two tailors and a draper were to be found at 111, 105, and 93-95. A grocer, a general dealer, two watchmakers and a coffeehouse keeper complete the picture for the north side. On the south side, the Co-op, having moved into its present premises in 1875, offered groceries, drapery, hardware, boots, and shoes. Alexander Ellis had his chemists on the corner.

By 1911 the population growth had slowed and had reached 4691 males and 4258 females. Skelton had become a stable and thriving community, its High Street now filled with shops. The section of the High Street discussed here would have felt quite familiar if we could travel back in time. On the site of what is now The Amber Rooms, 79 High Street, widow Margaret Clay ran the Stationers and Newsagent business established by her late husband. She was also enumerated as being the Telephone Exchange operator. The exchange would, almost certainly, have been established at 15 High Street, where the telegraph office was located. She was no doubt helped by her two unmarried daughters who eked out a living producing 'Art Needlework', nowadays the domain of many hobbyists.

Dressmakers, tailors, and needlewomen were dotted along the High Street. In the days before off the peg clothing, people had clothes made for them, made their own outfits, or wore second-hand. Tailor Emile Parvass, a German, lived at number 83 with his wife, a dressmaker, and two sons. One wonders if attitudes to him changed with the outbreak of

WW1. Further along at 107 we find John Lightfoot Taylor, a draper and grocer, and two doors along at 111 is John Wood, another tailor, assisted by his wife. At 115 Jane Dowson, a 71-year-old widow, was dressmaking, together with her daughter-in- law Amy Small. Yet another Grocer and Draper, widower Henry Hodge was aided and assisted by his two daughters at number 125.

Now to take a closer look at the shoppers. The housewives who appeared on the census forms from 1881 to 1911 would find the idea of artificial tans and false nails a bizarre concept. Life was hard, their housework labour intensive. Coal had to be carried, fires lit for hot water, toilets consisted of an earth closet in the back alley or yard, and bathing was done in a tin bath. Homes were lit with oil lamps and baking and cooking done on a range.

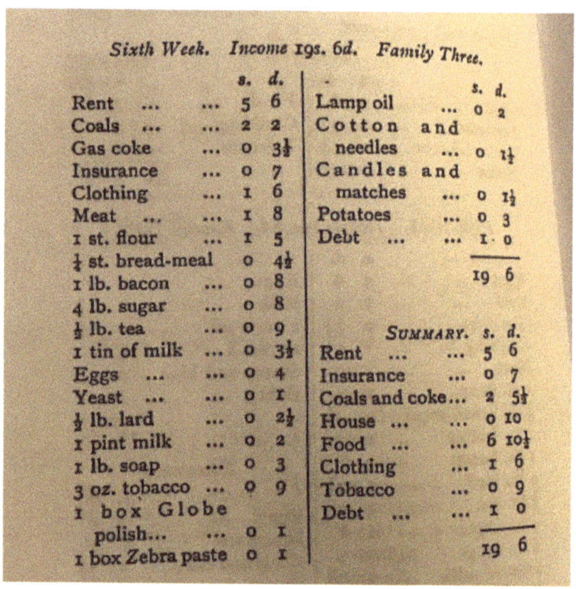

Sixth Week. Income 19s. 6d. Family Three.

	s.	d.
Rent	5	6
Coals	2	2
Gas coke ...	0	3½
Insurance ...	0	7
Clothing ...	1	6
Meat	1	8
1 st. flour ...	1	5
½ st. bread-meal	0	4½
1 lb. bacon ...	0	8
4 lb. sugar ...	0	8
½ lb. tea ...	0	9
1 tin of milk ...	0	3½
Eggs	0	4
Yeast	0	1
½ lb. lard ...	0	2½
1 pint milk ...	0	2
1 lb. soap ...	0	3
3 oz. tobacco ...	0	9
1 box Globe polish... ...	0	1
1 box Zebra paste	0	1
Lamp oil ...	0	2
Cotton and needles ...	0	1½
Candles and matches ...	0	1½
Potatoes ...	0	3
Debt	1	0
	19	6

Summary.	s.	d.
Rent	5	6
Insurance ...	0	7
Coals and coke...	2	5½
House	0	10
Food	6	10½
Clothing ...	1	6
Tobacco ...	0	9
Debt	1	0
	19	6

Chart of household expenditure from Florence Bell's *At the Works*, p.60.

Cars and fridges belonged to the future; food had to be either grown, with eggs and fresh vegetables coming from the family allotment, made at home, or bought fresh every day. Shops had to be nearby, although street traders such as the milkman and coal man supplemented the availability of goods.

A glimpse into this world is offered in a survey of working-class life amongst the families of Middlesbrough Iron workers. One section offers a fascinating insight into the weekly budgets of the housewives who had to count every ha'-penny. In the example shown opposite, the sixth week of shopping for a small family of three on a varied weekly income from 18s 6d to £1 3s 9d, we find the rent is hefty, 5s 6d. Insurance, probably paid into the Co-op, was 7d, heating and light – coal, coke gas, candles, matches, lamp oil - came to 2s 15½d. Cleaning materials came to 5d but the housewife may have had some from previous weeks. The husband had a generous 9d for tobacco, but this seems the only luxury. Vegetables, apart from potatoes, are absent from the shopping list, as the families would grow their own on allotments. We can surmise from this that potatoes made up a large part of meals which is why the allotment provision needed supplementing. The diet is limited. There is the means to make bread and other baking– flour, yeast, eggs, a rather large quantity of sugar, 4lb, and the tea for which much of it was destined. A tin of milk was condensed milk which went into mugs of tea and was spread on bread. One pint of milk was bought from the shop, the rest probably from the milk cart. Finally, meat and bacon make up the week's groceries. We find butter and lard had made an appearance in earlier weeks and currants were bought in week one. This diet was supplemented by the vegetables and eggs from the allotment, previously mentioned, which may well have contained a pig to be fattened and slaughtered. A few rabbits and possibly poached pheasants supplemented the shopping. Money was tight and new clothes appear rarely. A pair of boots was purchased for 5s 11d on the week of the best wage - £1 3s 9d – but this item accounted for a quarter of the week's income. Otherwise 'clothing' accounts for 1s to 1s 6d per week – this could be anything from corset stays to knitting wool, or material bought from the drapers. Most families went into debt which had to be repaid weekly.

72 High Street in 1875 (top),1901 (left) & 2019 (right)

Having described the changes in the High Street brought about through industrialisation and social change, and examined the budget of a working family, we will now look in some detail at three of the shops involved in the refurbishment scheme, and explore the lives of those who lived in them.

Alexander Ellis, Dispensing Chemist

Alexander Ellis, chemist and druggist, was born in Dublin in 1842. Little is known of his early life due to a fire destroying many Irish documents. The first record of him in Skelton was on the 1871 census that shows he married a Skelton girl. His wedding certificate of 1866 shows his bride was called Bessy Stobbs. The pair had seven children in rapid succession. In 1871 they are recorded as living in Main Street – houses were not numbered until 1881, by which time Main Street had become the High Street and the large corner building they lived in was 72 , now Hair Expressions. The building dates from around 1870, so Alexander, Bessy and their growing family were most likely the first occupants.

Alexander Ellis was a member of the Pharmaceutical Society of Great Britain. Founded in 1841, its purpose was *'advancing chemistry and pharmacy and promoting a uniform system of education for the protection of those who carry on the business of chemists and druggists'.* This brought regulation to a hitherto unregulated industry, in which anyone could sell drugs and claim to be a pharmacist. In 1872 a Pharmacy Act decreed that anyone who wanted to run a Dispensing Chemists had to be a member of this society.

Ellis was one of the respectable 'middle class' of Skelton, his membership of the Pharmaceutical Society giving him status, although in 1876 his veneer slipped when he was fined one shilling for letting his dog run loose for a fortnight. His wife, Bessy, was from a working-class family. On her and Alexander's wedding certificate her father, George Stobbs, was described as a railway labourer. This labourer was, however, upwardly mobile and by 1871 was an under steward at one of the Skelton mines. He then became a Housing Land Agent. By 1881 at the age of 68 he is recorded on the census as working as a Farm Bailiff and his residence was listed as Belle Villa, now Hill View in Skelton.

The same 1881 census shows that Alexander Ellis was equally upwardly mobile and had expanded his business. Now he was not only a Druggist, but a Registrar of Births and Deaths, Vaccinations Officer, and Postmaster. He dealt with the post and money orders which enabled those without bank accounts, i.e. most of the population, to buy goods and services by post. He was able to send Telegraphs and ran a Post Office Savings Bank. Unlike today, there were two mail deliveries. Letters were sorted at 5.30 in the morning, ready for the first delivery at 9.30 am, the second being at 6.30 pm. In 1881 three of the Ellis family worked in the shop. Frances Anne dealt with the sale of stationery, and books, Jenny assisted her father as assistant postmaster while Alice was in charge of the telegrams. By 1893 Frances Anne had her own stationers at 77 High Street, now the Co-op Funeral Parlour.

Alexander Ellis' role as Registrar fitted perfectly with his job as Vaccinations Officer. The Vaccination Act of 1853 made vaccination against smallpox compulsory, and from 1872 it became a legal requirement to register a birth. The Registrar had to inform the Vaccinations Officer of a registered birth and the child had to be vaccinated within three to four months, or the parents would be fined one pound.

Those of us born before 1950 would probably recognise some of the goods for sale in the chemists of the late 1800s such as Veno's Cough Mixture, Owbridge's Lung Tonic and the numerous laxatives that were deemed to act as a 'tonic', such as Epsom Salts. Families lined their children up on a Friday night for a dose of Castor Oil or California Syrup of Figs. Some drugs became illegal, namely laudanum, which was in Ellis' time freely dispensed. Kelly's directory of 1888 refers to an incident on the 18th of July in which a young girl bought three penny worth of laudanum at the Skelton Chemist from a Miss Ellis, one of the Ellis' daughters, claiming it was for her employer. It transpired that the girl had been sacked from her place of employment, and, fearing she would be sent to the Guisborough workhouse, drank the laudanum in one go. Rather like taking paracetamol nowadays, one dose dulled the pain, a bottle full could kill. The laudanum drinker recovered from poisoning, but back in 1888, attempting suicide was a crime. The unfortunate girl was tried at York Assizes, sent to a 'home for her safe keeping' and given a nominal one hour's imprisonment.

As the 19th century ended, Number 72 High Street was established as the Chemists and Post Office many of us remember. Ellis retired, having sold the business to Walter Wright Kingston, who was described on the 1901 census as a Chemist Dealer and Sub Postmaster. The Kingston family ran the business until 1995. The changeover will have coincided with the moment in 1897 when Post Offices throughout the country were issued with bicycles enabling their staff, i.e. the postmen and paper boys, to speed up their delivery, and Skelton's Post Office was no exception.

Sadly, Bessy Ellis died in July 1891 and in 1894 Alexander Ellis married a spinster from Newcastle with inherited wealth, her father having made his money as a chemist and a physician. The family moved on masse to Newcastle where Alexander died in 1906. He was brought back to Skelton to be buried.

J L Taylor

In 1901, no.105 High Street (now The Ark) was John Lightfoot Taylor's grocery and drapery shop. This shop had moved from Boosbeck Road and now competed with other grocers and drapers, including the Co-op, that were dotted along the High Street. The family lived next door at 107, (now Skelton Opticians). On the 1901 census the household consisted of John Lightfoot Taylor (1861-1945), his wife Alice Hannah Taylor, née Emmerson (1863-1907), and a servant, Elizabeth McGee. John and Alice are buried in Skelton cemetery; their headstone tells us that John Taylor was a chorister for sixty-nine years at All Saints, Skelton. The Taylors were clearly a respectable couple.

105 High Street: John L Taylor's shop

105/107 High Street awaiting renovation
The Ark & Skelton Opticians

John Lightfoot Taylor was originally from Normanby, near Fylingdales. The son of a farmer, he first appears in Skelton on the 1881 census, at the age of 20, working and living at Cleveland House, a shop and residential property next door to the Duke William. He was a draper's apprentice, employed by Thomas Taylor, grocer and draper, possibly a family member. Thomas Taylor was also a Wesleyan preacher, so John was part of a deeply religious household. Ten years later John was still at Cleveland House but had a new master, Alfred Harris, who is described on the 1891 census as a Draper, Grocer and Dressmaker.

John branched out on his own shortly after this. In 1894, an advert for flour tells us that it could be bought at J L Taylors, of Boosbeck Road. Where did John get the money to buy his first shop? Could Alice Emmerson, who he married in 1897, have helped him? Alice was one of four children brought up by their great aunt and uncle, sister and brother Hannah and Stephen Emmerson. Alice remained as Aunt Hannah's companion until the old lady died at the age of 93. It is not known when she began 'courting' John Lightfoot Taylor, but it may well have been a long, drawn out, courtship. Perhaps they met at church. Alice's family were churchwardens and John joined All Saint's choir when he was just 17. Alice, too, may have been in the choir, one of the few choirs to have their female members wearing surplices. The Emmersons were not short of money and when Uncle Stephen died in 1887, he left Alice a house in William Street, North Skelton, which she sold to George King, watchmaker, whose premises were on the site of Skelton Deli. Through the 1890s the couple continued to live apart, Alice looking after Aunt Hannah and John running his shop and singing in the choir on Sunday.

1897 was a momentous year for the pair. Aunt Hannah finally died in May at the age of 93, leaving Alice £200, three feather beds and a mountain of crockery and cutlery, so we can assume she was anticipating Alice's marriage. The couple wed four months later, on the 27th September, when Alice was 32 and John was 36. But not in All Saints Skelton. The couple were married at the imposing church of St Ignatius in Sunderland. This was puzzling until we find that the church was built and funded by a former Bishop of Durham, The Reverend Joseph Barber Lightfoot, a cousin, or uncle, of the bridegroom. It must have been a great honour for John and Alice. The Bishop had previously taught at Cambridge University, researched and written several acclaimed books on theology, and in 1861 was appointed chaplain, (one of many) to Prince Albert and Queen Victoria. A chapel and a stained-glass window at Auckland Castle (the official residence of the Bishops of Durham) are dedicated to Bishop Lightfoot. It seems that John and Alice, as well as being deeply religious, were somewhat status conscious.

Once married, the couple returned to Skelton to the more mundane task of running their grocery and draper's which John had relocated to 105 and 107 High Street. Again, was it Alice's money that enabled *this* move?

In the days before the advent of off-the-peg clothing, clothes would either be second hand or people made their own, so a draper would be guaranteed customers as the many drapers in Skelton High Street in 1901 demonstrate. The shop and its contents would not be vastly different to similar outlets in the nineteen forties and fifties which many of us remember. We will also remember the housewives' obsession with cleaning. John and Alice would sell products such as Globe Polish, a paste guaranteeing gleaming 'brasses', Zebra Polish, a black paste for cleaning the grate, Gold Dust washing powder, 'Blue' a powder to add to the white wash to enhance the whiteness, and, of course, the bath brick or donkey stone for scrubbing the front door step.

The couple were only married ten years. Their firstborn, a son, died three months after his birth in 1898. Another son born in 1903 and twin girls born in 1906, survived, but were only four and one when Alice died in 1907. The five-year age gap between her sons might suggest miscarriages, but this apart Alice was forty when her twins were born and probably died of exhaustion.

John remarried in the first quarter of 1910, his need for a childminder probably all-consuming. At the time of the 1911 census John was 49 and had been married just over a year. His new young wife, Ethel Smith, was 29 and from his hometown of Fylingdales, so perhaps was either a distant relative or from a neighbouring family. Living with them was Alice's niece Elizabeth.

The pair remained married until John's death in 1943 when he joined Alice in Skelton cemetery. Ethel had no children, but she brought up three stepchildren and died in 1986 at her home on South Terrace, where she presumably moved when she retired from the grocery and drapery business. Her name appears on the family headstone beneath those of John and Alice -almost as an afterthought.

E.M. Blair

Mrs Blairs Wool and Baby Boutique, (formerly E.M. Blair), was owned by Elsie May Blair, a familiar face to many Skelton residents over the fifty odd years she ran the shop. Her daughter, Jean Crocker, continues the family tradition. Jean's wedding photograph, taken in 1985, shows the shop as it was. Elsie Blair, elegant in pale pink, stands in the doorway. The photograph below shows the shop today, post renovation.

115 High Street after renovation

The shop is situated at 115 High Street. It makes its first appearance as a residence on the 1881 census. Living there were John Cornforth, Cordwainer [shoemaker], Jane, his wife, and their two daughters aged three and one. Ten years later we find James Scott and his wife in residence. Scott is described as a 'stationary engineer' on the 1881 census. He maintained the mechanism that drove the lift shaft in the mine, and its winding gear is now depicted on the mosaic below the main shop window. Ten years later, in 1901, George Dowson, a check weigher at the mine, and family were living at no 115. By 1911 George had died and his widow, Jane Dowson, with her daughter-in-law Amy Small, were 'working from home' earning their living as dressmakers.

Twenty-eight years later, the 1939 Register records that living at 115 were Herman Southgate, his wife Emily (née Blyth), and Emily's sister, Eva Blyth. Eva is described as a 'drapery shop keeper', (because 115 was now a shop) whilst Emily's employment is described as 'shop attendant/unpaid domestic duties'. She helped Eva and ran the house. Herman, described as a 'Traveller (with own drapery)', was a travelling salesman. Who were these three people?

Eva and Emily were the two youngest of nine children belonging to Edgar Blyth and his wife Elizabeth, who arrived in Skelton from Stowmarket in Suffolk shortly after their marriage in 1876. Edgar would most likely have been an agricultural worker seeking work in the Ironstone mines. He found work as a platelayer, being still employed in this capacity in 1911 at the age of 62. By 1911 Emily was also working outside the home as an Elementary school teacher, whereas Eva, who was disabled, was confined to the home. The Blyth family moved several times, from 5 East Terrace to 95 High Street and thence to 20 Dixon Street.

In 1922 the sisters were running number 115 as a sweet shop under the name of Blyth's, so Emily must have given up teaching. She eventually married Herman Southgate in 1928 when she was 42 and he was 40, and the shop became a draper's. But who was Herman? The name 'Herman' is hardly one from East Cleveland. Mrs Blair understood that he was a German Jew who had come to England to escape the persecution of the Jews in Germany and had naturalized his surname. This would make for exciting reading - but in fact Herman was from Ipswich. Perhaps his mother was German? Definitely not! Her surname was Smith. Military records show that Herman was a Lance Bombardier in the Royal Horse and Royal Field Artillery during World War I, attacking Germans rather than being one of them.

The Southgates possibly changed their shop's function from confectioners to drapers when they married, and it remained the domain of Emily and her sister, Eva. Herman, recognisable by his black, bushy moustache, drove around the East Cleveland villages and the moors selling ladies underwear and dressmaking materials. We know little about the trio, only snippets of information. One Skelton resident remembers Emily as being 'a very nice woman'. Herman does not seem to have had many DIY skills. Jean Crocker remembers her mother complaining that most jobs done by him were botched. Jean also remembers that the Southgates had a rudimentary bathroom. A room had been stripped bare and a tin bath placed in the centre of it.

Other Skelton residents can remember Blyth's in the early 1950s when, due to the austerity caused by World War II, nothing much had changed in terms of available goods. We can imagine the rest from museum reconstructions such as Beamish. Knitting wool of course, sewing materials, and a range of necessities for the home and for oneself. Antimacassars for the back of armchairs to soak up men's hair oil, shaving brushes and strops, collar stiffeners, armlets to shorten the arms of shirts, buttons and thread, lace cuffs and collars, corset stays, liberty bodices, flannel vests and underwear, baby clothes including bibs and nappies, cot quilts sheets and blankets – the list is endless.

Jean Crocker remembers her mother telling her that the Blyth's were heavily involved in a Mission which she believed met in a building belonging to the shop, in the alleyway behind it. So far research has not revealed any more about this, apart from one Skelton resident who has a faint recollection of a Plymouth Brethren sect operating in Skelton.

Elsie Blair saw that Blyth's was for sale when she and her husband were house hunting in Skelton, and she bought it in 1959. Elsie was not too sure that she wanted to run a shop. She had always worked, as a typist and book-keeper, and now wanted to be at home with young Jean. Her husband persuaded her otherwise, suggesting that the shop would provide security should anything happen to him and, working from home, she could still be with her little girl. Blyth's was duly bought, its name changed to E.M. Blair, and the Southgates retired to Ipswich, Herman's childhood home. Jean grew up above the shop, often playing near her mum as she served customers, as did her own daughter and son, many years later.

The interior layout remained much the same until the recent renovation, so most Skelton residents will remember the shop as it was. Sadly, Elsie Blair's husband died three years after they bought Blyth's, so the shop did provide her with a lifeline and a living. She was a familiar, friendly face in the shop until 6 weeks before she died at the age of 84.

This chapter has discussed the changing face of shopping in Skelton. The growth and development of the central section of the High Street, and the shopping habits of the miners' wives, were described followed by a closer look at the history of three of the shops involved in the reconstruction scheme.

Whilst we in the 21st Century would be able to recognise the Skelton High Street of the late Victorian era; the residents back then would be amazed at the High Street's transformation. They would find it hard to grasp the ways in which their High Street has evolved from a place where shopping was a necessity to a venue lined with trees and flower tubs – a place where shopping has now become a pleasurable leisure pursuit.

The mosaic mural

Peter Appleton

This large mosaic mural depicts episodes from the history of the village of Skelton-in-Cleveland. The elements of the design are laid out in a timeline that runs from left to right. However, to produce a visually satisfying finished product, some elements appear slightly out of their proper chronological order.

Domesday Book

Starting at the extreme left we have the Domesday Book. This can be thought of as England's first national census. It was commissioned in December 1085 by order of William the Conqueror. He needed to assess the wealth and assets of his subjects, and the state of the country's economy in the aftermath of the Conquest and the unrest that followed it. Lacking this knowledge, he was unable to set a level for the taxation with which to pay for his army. Therefore, a survey was set in motion, the results being published in 1086. Skelton gets a couple of mentions in it.

> *"In Skelton, the Count of Mortain [has] 13 carucates."*

> *"In Skelton [are] 13 carucates to the geld, and there could be 7 ploughs. Uhtræd had 1 manor there. Now Richard has it of the Count. In demesne [is] 1 plough; and 12 villans with*

> *3 ploughs, and 20 acres of meadow. [There is] woodland pasture 2 leagues long and 2 furlongs broad. The whole manor [is] 5 leagues long and 2 broad. In the time of Edward the King [it was] worth 40s; now 16s."*

Those two quotes from Domesday Book include terms that are likely to be unfamiliar to many readers. Here are explanations:

- Carucate – An area of land equal to the amount that could be worked by a team of eight oxen.
- Demesne – Land in the personal possession of a Lord, used to support that Lord rather than the tenants working it.
- Furlong – A unit of measure equal to the length of a ploughed furrow.
- Geld – A tax based on land area.
- League – a measure of distance, 1000 paces in length, or roughly 1½ Roman miles. In later medieval times the league was equal to 12 furlongs, whereas the mile was standardized at 8 furlongs. Subsequently the league became standardized at three miles.
- Villans - The nominally free inhabitants of a village.

Arms of de Brus

The blue lion rampant is the arms of the de Brus family. Robert de Brus became lord of the manor of Skelton when Henry became king of England, in August 1100.

Medieval ox plough

Oxen, castrated male cattle, were used extensively in medieval times as draught animals, pulling carts and ploughs. A measure of length, still used today in horse racing, is the furlong (= 220 yards). Its name started as "Furrow long" being the length of furrow that a pair of oxen could plough before they needed to take a breather.

Skelton Castle

The edifice we see today was built between 1785 and 1815 or thereabouts. It occupies the land on which Robert de Brus erected his castle in around 1105-1115. That castle was subsequently modified by the Fauconbergs, Conyers and Trotters before being pulled down by John Hall Stevenson. The design is based on several variants supplied by Sir John Soane, the eminent London architect.

Lawn and daffodils

A reminder of the Daffodil Sunday events of the late twentieth century, which hold fond memories for the older inhabitants. Now, in the twenty-first century, and thanks to the generosity of the current owner of the castle, Anthony Wharton, the younger generation are storing away their own memories of this event.

Old All Saints Church

The church that we see today, standing amidst the gravestones in its churchyard, was built in 1785 and 1786. The condition of its predecessor, a church originally built in 1325, had become deplorable. It was, quite frankly, becoming unsafe to hold services within the ailing fabric of the old building. A petition to the archbishop of York was prepared:

"To the Most Reverend Father in God William by Divine Providence Lord Archbishop of York Primate of England and Metropolitan.

The Humble Petition of the Curate Churchwardens and Principal Parishioners and Inhabitants of the Parish of Skelton-in-Cleveland within your Grace's Diocese of York.

Sheweth That the Parish Church of Skelton aforesaid is very old and in a ruinous and decayed situation and cannot conveniently be repaired to make the same safe and secure from Danger, but must be wholly taken down and rebuilt (except the Chancel part of the said Church)..."

Following that, and in just over three weeks, the archbishop had appointed three local vicars to be a Commission of Enquiry, the three had visited the church, prepared and submitted their report, and the archbishop had issued the faculty (church-speak for planning permission). That speed of response is impressive. We couldn't achieve that today, with all the benefit of e-mail and telephone communication. To think, that all they had then were hand-written letters carried by a horse rider or on the horse-drawn coaches.

The new building was paid for by a £100 donation from the lord of the manor, Joseph William Hall Stevenson, subscriptions from the parishioners raised by purchasing their pews, and the sale, to the local plumber, of the lead removed from the old roof. In all, a total of £444 was raised which covered the cost of construction, £443.2s.7d and left a small profit, which was added to the church funds.

Daisies and butterflies

These serve as a reminder of how urban development can lead to loss of wildlife habitat. Sympathetic planting in gardens and open spaces can go some way to replacing the lost habitat but these are only islands in an ocean of roads and houses.

Ironstone miner carrying pickaxe and midge

The main seam of the Cleveland Ironstone was discovered in the Skinningrove valley in 1847. The next 40-50 years saw a vast change to East Cleveland. As mines were opened, communities sprang up to house the miners and their families. They came from the copper and tin mines of Cornwall, the coal mines of Wales and Scotland, and the farmlands of East Anglia.

The pickaxe would have been used to give the miner a pilot hole in which to set his drill when preparing the face for the next round of blasting.

In his left hand, he is carrying his midge. This was a wooden box, in which he put his candle. The primary use of the midge was to shield the candle from the draught of air created by the ventilation of the mine – to stop it getting blown out! It could also be used as a stool on which to stand to gain extra height. As a stool, it could also be used by the miner to sit on while eating his bait (sandwiches). He had to take a little care doing this given the proximity of parts of his body to the hot flame of the candle! If his missus (wife) had cooked some pies and he had taken one as his bait, he could slip it in beside the candle to warm it gently while he worked.

High Street shops c.1900

The depiction of the north side of the High Street is based on old photographs and postcards. It shows how it looked in the last decade of the 19th century and first decade of the 20th century.

Wharton Arms

The façade gives us the date this pub was built - 1878. It opened originally as a hotel and included two large function rooms. During the Second World War, its cellar was modified to become an operation centre for the British Underground movement that would have formed in the event of a successful invasion by the German forces.

This building replaced a previous "Wharton Arms" that had occupied the site where now stands the Fire Station. Prior to becoming the Wharton Arms, the predecessor had been known as "The Board".

Home Farm cottages

A brief study of the bricks of these cottages and the "Wharton Arms" reveals that they are clearly of the same overall design. Thus, we can date these cottages to the late-1870s or early-1880s. They were part of the re-development of the Skelton Castle estates that was being financed by the royalties from the ironstone mining. The "Home Farm" of an estate would have been the "show farm" to which visiting dignitaries would have been taken to see the latest farming practices and equipment in use. Behind these cottages once stood a complete range of buildings: cow byres, horse stables, barns, etc. Some of these were stone built and dated from the early-17th century. Others were architect-designed and constructed using the same bricks as the cottages: a true "show farm".

All Saints parish church

This Grade II* listed building was dedicated in 1884. It was designed by the Newcastle architect Robert J Johnson and is built of stone from local Skelton quarries as well as from that at Aislaby, near Whitby. A new, larger church was required to accommodate the increase in congregation brought on by the migration into the area of the ironstone miners and their families.

The church contains many features of interest and is well worth a visit. Of note are the two memorials to those parishioners who were killed during World War 1. On the wall of the north aisle is the parish's Roll of Honour plaque, whilst the great west window incorporates, in its stained glass, imagery reflecting all aspects of the war: on land, at sea and in the air.

Cart with milk churns, pulled by Cleveland Bay horse

Even in the early 1960s, door-to-door milk deliveries were still taking place from churns transported on a two-wheeled cart pulled by a pony. On the mural, a little artistic licence has been allowed and the pony has been replaced by that equine icon of our area – the Cleveland Bay.

Swift flying in sky

The sound of swifts screaming over the High Street has been a familiar summer sound for centuries. Modern housing and improvement to older properties are reducing the available nest sites. For how many years will we continue to hear them?

Co-op building behind the horse

This building was taken over by the Skelton Co-operative Society in 1875. The concept of the Co-operative, at that time, was that it was an organisation owned and run by the ironstone miners for the benefit of their families. The final section of this book gives more information.

War Memorial

The War Memorial was unveiled on Armistice Day 1921. The costs were covered by public subscriptions and the names were put forward by relatives of the fallen. The land was given by W.H.A. Wharton.

Cleveland Way fingerpost

The Cleveland Way was the second National Trail to be established in England (after the Pennine Way). It was officially opened on 24th May 1969 and runs for 110 miles, from Helmsley to Filey Brigg. The route is horseshoe-shaped, running around the western edge of the North York Moors National Park and along the cliff tops of the North Sea coast.

Skelton sits astride this route. The farm track from Airy Hill brings the walkers into Skelton Green. From there, the field paths lead them onto the heights overlooking the village and the vista of the Tees Bay. The flight of steps from The Hills brings them past Ringrose Orchard and into the High Street. A short urban stretch takes them down Coniston Road, Derwent Road and Windermere Drive before taking them through the underpass at the A174 road and into the woods for their onward journey into Saltburn.

Whipping Post

This has been a source of much debate amongst the Victorian antiquarians and previous generations of local historians. Some claim it was the village whipping post, others that it is only the shaft of the old market cross. What's my opinion? Well, the metal fittings near the top of the post do resemble, in both appearance and position, fittings that are depicted on a sketch of a whipping post that can be seen at the Police Museum in Ripon. Have a look at our post, then go visit the Police Museum, and make up your own mind on this matter.

Fruit tree

This brings us into the 21st century and represents the Ringrose Orchard. This wonderful park, garden and orchard was created out of abandoned allotments that were being rapidly re-colonised by shrubs, trees, brambles, and nettles. A small band of volunteers worked tirelessly to clear the site. They then produced a design for the hard landscaping and the planting scheme. Finally, they set about turning their dream into reality.

Children dancing round a May Pole

This, and the next two are interlinked. In the 1950s, and possibly later, it was the tradition that, on the first school day on or after May 1st, the children from the Infants School would gather on the village green and celebrate May Day (1st May) by performing dances round the May Pole. Although the grass would have been cut a few days beforehand, it was usually covered with daisies.

Infants School behind the dancers

How many generations of little children started their education in this building? The building was provided to meet the requirements of laws passed in the mid-Victorian period: the Education Acts of 1870 and 1875. It closed as a school following the opening of Skelton Primary School, on Station Lane, at Hollybush, but its life with the little ones continued when, for a time, it became a Nursery.

Daises in front of the dancers

In spring and early summer, the village green grows a lovely carpet of daisies.

Long-sword dancer

In many respects, the "sword dance" was a traditional folk dance in the mining communities of northern England. In the coal mining districts of Durham, the sword was short, flexible, had handles at both ends, and was known as a rapper. In the Yorkshire area, whether in coal mining or ironstone mining communities, the sword was long, stiff and had a handle at one end only. The dancers formed a ring, each holding the point of the next dancer's sword, and then performed complex circling and inter-weaving manoeuvres, stepping over swords held low, and ducking under swords held high, and without letting go of the swords. The dance culminated with the interlocking of all the swords into the "lock", at which point the swords were held aloft for all to see.

Tub planter

The planter represents all the hard work done by the members of Skelton Villages Civic Pride, raising money to finance these planters and the hanging baskets that are such a colourful feature of our village.

Ornamental pear tree

The tall, slender tree at the extreme right of the mural represents the commitment of Redcar & Cleveland Borough Council to the Townscape project. They carried out the first phase of the project, to the commercial core of the High Street, with improvements to the public realm, i.e. the street furniture, paving, and five ornamental trees. The variety of tree chosen was selected because its roots do not spread, they go deep, in a mirror-image of the above ground growth. Thus, damage to the foundations of the buildings and underground services is avoided.

Boroughgate

Peter Appleton

Background

Growing up from childhood in the village, I was very much aware of the long history that it had. I knew about the de Brus family building the first castle. As a pupil at Guisborough Grammar School, I learned that Robert Pursglove, last prior of Gisborough priory had founded the school in 1561. I also learned that Robert de Brus, founder of Skelton castle, had founded the Priory. Looking around my village, I could tell that some of the buildings were centuries old but not of medieval date. The question that formed in my mind, as an enquiring teenager, was: "whereabouts had the medieval community of Skelton been situated?".

In the summer of 1969, I participated in an amateur-led dig in Bagdale field, which lies to the east of Boroughgate field. That was just one season of four or five which attempted to obtain evidence of the medieval settlement of Skelton. Sufficient dateable finds came out of the excavation to confirm that there was a nearby community, but it became clear that we were not digging on it. On the periphery, yes, but not in the centre of the community. "Where was medieval Skelton?" was still an unanswered question.

Ever since, the hope of getting the answer had lingered. When Skelton History Group was formed in July 2012, one of our first discussions was around the question: "What projects would we like to run?" Top of that list was an archaeological investigation of Boroughgate. However, we knew we would need to set a track record of successful smaller projects before applying for funds to carry out such an investigation. I resigned myself to continue waiting for the answer. After all, I had already waited over forty years; I could wait a few more.

Then, in 2014, Joyce White told me about the inclusion within the proposed Townscape Heritage project of a 3-year programme of archaeological investigation in the Boroughgate field. If the project got its funding, it looked certain that I would get an answer to my question. The project did get its funding and the 3-year programme of archaeological investigation took place. Did I get the answer? Read on...

The site

The site comprises two fields that lie on the western edge of Skelton, between the Guisborough to Skelton road and Back Lane Farm.

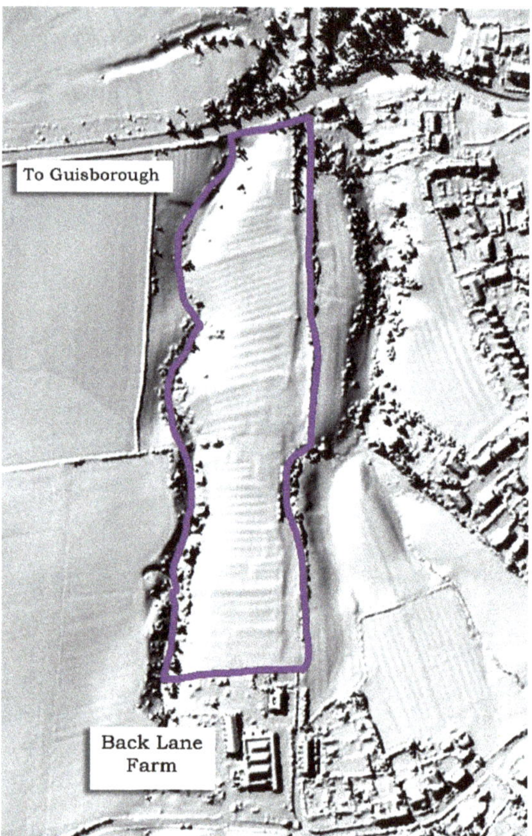

They are bounded on the west by Lawns Gill. At their eastern edge is the hollow way known as Boroughgate Lane.

The image opposite is a LIDAR image of the site. This technology reveals the presence of features that don't always show on photographs.

Season 1 – Geophysical surveys

The first season, from 2nd to 11th November 2016, involved professional archaeologists from Archaeology Services Durham University. Their objective was *"to assess the nature and extent of any sub-surface features of potential archaeological or historic significance"* in the two fields that comprised the study area. Two techniques were chosen: geomagnetic and earth electrical resistance surveys. Both techniques enable the identification of sub-surface features such as walls, ditches, and pits.

GPS was used to establish a grid of 20m squares across the two fields (total area was about 4 hectares). The grid was then systematically surveyed by the professionals, walking over it, carrying hand-held magnetometers. For this survey it was vital that no metal objects of any kind came near to the magnetometers.

The earth electrical resistance survey came next. For this, it was possible to get some of the volunteers involved.

The results of the surveys confirmed expectations. There was clear evidence of revetments dividing the fields into plots and similar revetments along the western edge of the hollow way. Some of the plots in the southern field showed evidence of internal dividing structures.

Season 2 – Earthwork survey

The second season, from 9th to 19th May 2017, saw a team of volunteers, led by Tees Archaeology personnel, carry out a survey of the "humps and bumps" which formed a very visible feature within the field. The first day was bitterly cold, but thereafter the sun shone, and the weather turned much milder.

The stile at the northern entrance to the field was chosen as the datum point for the GPS. Further GPS points, taken as offsets from the datum, were used to create a base line running along the top of the western boundary of the hollow-way. A surveyor's tape was then laid along this.

The changes in slope were identified and marked with small flags and then the positions carefully measured, using a second surveyor's tape, and manually plotted onto graph paper at a scale of 1:100.

Levelled profiles were also taken and manually drawn on graph paper. As you might gather, it was a very labour-intensive operation.

Once you started looking at the "humps and bumps" in this systematic way, it was possible to identify the approximate dimensions of potential buildings and, in some cases, the position of the doorways into them. It became clear that there were different plot sizes in each field. Those in the northern field were typically twice as large as those in the southern field. Also, they were aligned on a southwest - northeast axis, whereas those in the southern field were aligned west-east. In all cases, their frontages were presumed to lie parallel with the hollow way.

An excavation strategy was developed by the staff of Tees Archaeology. This brought together all the now available information: historic documentary sources, reports of the 1969-1972 seasons of amateur-led excavation in the adjoining field, aerial photographs and LIDAR images, plus the two survey reports from 2016 and 2017: one geophysical and one earthwork. Pooling all the above information, the locations for four trenches were identified: two in the north field, and two in the south field. These were assigned the letters A-D, reading from south to north.

Season 3 – Archaeological excavation

Season three, from 25th June to 6th July 2018, saw the excavation itself take place during the hottest two weeks of that summer. Temperatures were above 25°C for the entire fortnight, and there was no shade out in the open of the fields. It was almost too hot and keeping hydrated was essential for everybody.

The selection of images which follow gives some idea of what happened and what was found.

Trench B: The boundary wall of a property

Our metal detectorist working over the spoil heap

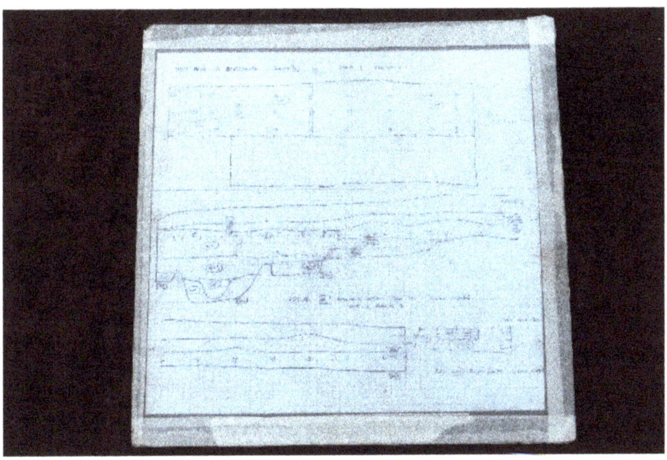

Trench C: Detailed plans and sections

Sunday 1st July 2018 was the Open Day, when members of the public were shown around the site.

In these two images of trench A, one of the professional archaeologists explains the significance of the finds to interested groups. The line of pad stones across this trench are clearly visible. Each of these would have supported a timber that formed part of the structure of the building. The large pad stone in the foreground was matched by one at the far side. These would probably have supported the "cruck" frames.

The distance between the large pads was six metres. For comparison, Stang End cruck house at Ryedale Folk Museum has pads 4.5 metres apart.

Every item that came out of the ground had to be washed and labelled. Quite often, the removal of the soil revealed previously hidden details such as patterns made by thumbprints, or the colours left by the glaze.

Most of the pottery dated to the 12th and 13th centuries.

Glazed pot rim

Glazed jug handle in barley sugar twist design

Decorated pot rim

Typical East Cleveland ware pot rim

But the finest piece of pottery was from a much later date. This ornate clay pipe bowl, in the design of a fish, with a piece of blue glass for an eye, and a mermaid reclining against the base of the bowl, was tentatively dated to the 18th or early-19th century. We were left wondering how an item with such obvious nautical connections found its final resting place in Boroughgate field.

Conclusion

The original primary objective had been to determine whether the humps and bumps in the Boroughgate field were the remains of an early settlement at Skelton, as was generally believed. We can now state, with certainty, that they were.

Could we assign a definite date to the settlement? From the dates assigned to the pottery finds, we can assert that the settlement existed during the 12th and 13th centuries.

The LIDAR images and the earthwork survey both indicated that the plots in the field were of two different sizes and on two different alignments. Was this because they were of different periods? That remains an open question, but the pottery did not support any difference in the dates. The date range of the pottery from trenches C & D (the northern ones) was not significantly different from that of the pottery from trenches A & B (the southern ones).

Why did the settlement not prosper? That is a matter for historical research rather than archaeological research. A combination of factors was probably responsible. In 1216, the castle was besieged by King John and his army. Perhaps they razed the community. The de Brus male line in Skelton died out in 1272 and the castle changed ownership. Perhaps the new owner didn't have the same commitment to the local community. And, of course, there would have been waves of plague and years of poor harvests leading to famine.

Personally, I had supported this archaeological investigation in the hope of getting an answer to that unanswered question: "Where was medieval Skelton?". Having tried to get an answer back in 1969, and failed, I now had the answer: at Boroughgate.

So, you see, it is true "Everything comes to he who waits". I just didn't expect to have to wait fifty years!

Medieval event

Derek Hedges

On Saturday 4th August 2018, an exciting medieval re-enactment took place in Skelton. The Heritage Project Team, always on the lookout for ideas, had considered Joyce and Stuart White's proposal of an historic sports day but none of the local teams felt able to commit to the idea, so it was back to the drawing board. Then Tony Harding, one of the key members of the team, came up with the notion of engaging a medieval re-enactment group. He thought *The Red Wyverns*, a group of enthusiastic volunteers, would fit the bill.

The Heritage Project Team decided that this event would link seamlessly with the archaeological dig and study of Boroughgate, Skelton's medieval settlement, which was to take place a few weeks earlier. Members were told that *The Red Wyverns* performed staged combat in full armour with medieval weapons and would set up a period encampment with a small forge and domestic kitchen. The Stockton Archery club and a wandering minstrel/jester added to the medieval atmosphere of the event. *The Red Wyverns* were awaited with excitement and anticipation... and they did not disappoint.

The Day

The day dawned bright and sunny and the event was officially opened in the marquee at 10:00am by John Haw, project manager for the Skelton Townscape project, who dedicated the event to the memory of Tony Harding who worked tirelessly and voluntarily in the Heritage Office, until his sudden death in April 2018, and who had been a major driving force behind the project.

Programme of Events

The Publicity Poster doubled as the Programme

The Marquee

Many local groups staged small exhibitions.

Skelton Villages Civic Pride

Skelton Townscape Heritage Project

Redcar & Cleveland Borough Council Community Development

Skelton History Group

Tees Archaeology

There was even an opportunity to try your hand at mosaic making.

By the end of the day, and thanks to all the many hands who made light work of the task, the mosaic was finished. A lasting feature of the Townscape Heritage project is a mosaic trail around the village. This one depicts the archaeological dig that took place in Boroughgate field during June and July 2018.

The Encampment

Medieval Kitchen (and not a Parmo in sight!)

"Wot", no Dishwasher!

Meeting the Wyverns

Strolling players
(Left) a medieval pop star: the hurdy-gurdy man
(Right) a medieval supermodel sporting the Jester look

Drill time

CHAAAARRGE!!!

You don't mess with a Wyvern if he gets annoyed with you!

Family feuding – Wyvern style!

Don't try this at home, kids

Archery was enjoyed by all Maid Marians and Robin Hoods
(and not a Kevin Costner in sight!)

The day was closed with the Trebuchet display.
Medieval artillery... or early form of air-mail delivery service?

Snapshot in Time

Margaret Drazin

Background

"Snapshot in Time" was the name given to the Buildings Recording activity of the Townscape Project. This activity was designed by Tees Archaeology and the running of it was overseen by Robin Daniels of Tees Archaeology.

For four successive years, volunteers spent a week in September exploring the streets of Skelton, armed with clipboards and cameras. Their task was to record details of every building in the conservation area. By doing so, they produced a record of what Skelton looks like now, and what its present appearance suggested about how it came to be as it is.

Volunteers, working mostly in pairs, were assigned a stretch of street frontage each day. They recorded, in detail, every building on that frontage, plus any associated buildings such as outhouses. The work was done entirely from the roadside footpaths unless a property owner invited entry onto their land.

The information captured on the recording forms and the digital images included: address, name or location; number of storeys; number and type of windows in each; number of type of entrances; the material used for the walls and roof; and any other points of detail that caught the eye. All elevations of the building were included, provided this was possible without trespass.

Those details gave clues to the original purpose and status of the building, and its later history. The accumulated history of the buildings and their occupants is, of course, the history of the settlement.

Now, this may sound like a dry academic exercise. It was far from it. Every day brought new encounters with householders and passers-by keen to know what was going on, and with a lively interest in their village and the history of their homes. Some residents came out a bit warily to see what was going on when people with clipboards showed up in front of their house. However, they quickly became engaged with the project and had lots to contribute. Many had lived in Skelton for a long time and were a fund of information and anecdote about both their own home and neighbouring properties. It was a vivid reminder that this activity was about appreciating the detail of a real place; a place for real people, lived in and adapted to their changing lives over many centuries.

There were also plenty of surprises in the buildings themselves when studied closely; some will be covered later in this chapter.

In most parts of the country, surviving domestic buildings from the 17th century and earlier are quite uncommon, and are rare from Tudor times and earlier. So, it was no surprise that there was little that was clearly dateable to the 18th century. At that time, like the rest of Cleveland, Skelton would have been, primarily, an agricultural village. All that is implied here is that the everyday domestic buildings were not built of durable materials.

The presence of a substantial late 18th century church building (Old All Saints church) indicates that some degree of prosperity had become well established. The old church has some medieval fabric in the chancel's north wall, indicating that there was a pre-existing building. The old church was strongly associated with the family at the castle but needed to serve villagers as well as the family and castle servants. For many centuries, as local landowners, the family would have been the major employers and, indeed, many of Skelton's buildings owe their origin directly to the successive owners of the castle and estate. Much of the older housing started life as 'tied' housing for estate workers. But there's also Hill House, a fine house of three bays, a classic 18th century design, perched above the old centre of the village on the south side of High Street.

What makes Skelton's townscape special?

The village combines a village green, a linear main street, and elevated footpaths. There are many villages that are built around a village green, and many that are built along a linear main street. Fewer have elevated footpaths. Skelton is unusual in having all three features.

But it is the main street that lies at the core of our village. Along its length it combines small shops with domestic dwellings. The architectural style is almost entirely vernacular, as building historians say. By this is meant that the properties have an identifiable local style, having been built by local craftsmen using local materials sourced from the local area.

If the village had grown to town size, larger, institutional buildings, both commercial and public, would have introduced more pompous and showy building styles in period fashions, and led to demolition of humbler domestic or agricultural buildings in the centre.

In Skelton there are no big florid banks and the surviving school buildings (now converted to other uses) are comparatively modest and unassertive. The larger buildings are, as usual, often those which are least harmonious with local traditions: the churches and chapels, and the fire station, for example. Much of the village, as we see it today, would be familiar to the first occupants of the many older properties which survive.

Along the principal axis of the High Street nearest the Green, small stone-built cottages, houses, and ex-shops predominate. This style continues up Green Road. Only a few, mostly commercial or public, buildings show frontages of red brick in this part of town. What does this tell us? Two things: It reminds us that for many centuries, bricks were hand-made and therefore not the cheap material they became with mass production; and good building stone was readily available, so it was widely used for ordinary domestic dwellings. There was extensive quarrying in Skelton itself, its legacy still visible along the hillsides to the south of the High Street. Some building stone would also have been a by-product of the earlier alum industry that was located at the eastern edge of the village.

Here and there around town are buildings faced with Pease bricks, as they're known. These whitish bricks were produced by the Pease & Partners company and used extensively in the Pease-developed resort of Saltburn-by-the-sea. Naturally, they were promoted as much as possible in the surrounding area.

They were principally produced at the Bankfoot plant at Crook near Durham, using products from the mining and chemical operations there, reminding us that the origins of the Pease's wealth began not in Yorkshire but in Durham.

Another distinctive material is similarly an industrial by-product. The attractive silver-grey surfaced bricks, or tiles, known as Scoria blocks, were produced from blast furnace slag. They were used to pave all the back streets of the terraced cottages and paved some yard entrances. They become a bit slippery in wet weather and are a nuisance to lift and re-lay when resurfacing roads. Therefore, many have been either taken up or covered over. A particularly fine set remains in the courtyard at the rear of the Wharton Arms, in this case proudly showing the trade name of the company that made them.

You can see from the uneven surface here that the setts can be high maintenance over a large area. Also, durable though they may be, they can be cracked by the heavy traffic of brewers' drays. However, they are attractive and desirable in smaller landscaping contexts, becoming quite sought-after. They come in different shapes, sizes, and surface patterns, and it's possible to see most of these if you keep your eyes open as you walk around in the villages and towns of Cleveland. If you are lucky enough to have any near or on your property, make the most of them!

The two materials just described show the extent of local business interests and their capacity for technical innovation, making the most of everything that their industrial operations made available to them, even their 'waste'. The Scoria block is visible proof that “where there’s muck, there’s brass”.

Having discussed the walls of the building and paving of the roads, what of the roof? Prior to the 18th century, thatch would have been the common roofing, either straw or heather. That would have been replaced by clay pantiles and, after the arrival of the railways, with Welsh or Lakeland slate. There were various small brick and tile works in the area; the one at Margrove Park probably the best known. There are no surviving thatched buildings in the village but there are certainly properties in the High Street with original pantile and original slate roofs of some antiquity. Keep your eyes open on your walks.

The Shape of Skelton

A walk from the old church to the parish church, from west to east along the main artery of the village, offers an opportunity to observe how the village has changed over the last two and a half centuries.

Like many settlements, the village developed around a crossroads of trade routes: a north-south one from the coast to the hinterland and an east-west one linking Stokesley and Whitby via several villages. This look at the village of today starts at the village green. Here we have a cluster of buildings, including two public houses. Entering the village from Skelton Ellers to the west we can try to imagine this road as a well-used track, a 'hollow way' worn deep by the hooves of carthorses pulling round the curving slope up to the green. The elevated footway on the north side of the road has been walled and fenced. This would have been a blessing to pedestrians when the track was muddy and unsurfaced. It's a distinctive village feature and there is a length of similar raised pavement up Green Road, and for the same reasons. Church Lane also has a raised path on its right leading to the church gate, although this is little used now.

Skelton did not develop into a chartered market town like Guisborough and so the green looks small and fragmented. However, the boundaries of the original village green are marked by the four lines of buildings: North Terrace, East Terrace, South Terrace and West Terrace. It was of a considerable size.

The old church is just out of sight down Church Lane, but its Rectory holds an imposing presence at the north-west corner of the green and with a former school, in a fine 19th century stone building, facing it. The two public houses, formerly operating as coaching inns with associated stabling, would have provided rooms and refreshment for the weary traveller. Methodist chapels can be glimpsed to the south of the crossroads where routes from Guisborough, through Loftus, to Whitby, and to the coast at Marske and Redcar, intersect. Hiding behind a hedge, between the public houses, is a rare surviving early shopfront (on a private house so to be viewed discreetly). All the elements of a traditional village nucleus are present.

The well-known architectural historian Nikolaus Pevsner came to Skelton while compiling the North Riding of Yorkshire volume of his monumental 'The Buildings of England' series. He describes Skelton as 'a big industrial village' - industrial wasn't a positive word then. It's hard to escape feeling that he was not entirely at home in the North East and perhaps didn't put his back into it in our local villages. Skelton had existed for many centuries before its 'industrial period', which lasted only about 100 years, and the only industry actually located within the old village was the quarrying along the slopes to the south of the High Street. The ironstone mines were scattered around in the neighbouring countryside.

The historic centre is typical of a medium-sized agricultural settlement with all the standard elements of a thriving farming and trading community. Although Home Farm has gone, Eggcup Farm, which probably preceded it in build date, remains almost opposite. The village used to have at least two abattoirs, essential in those days of local slaughter and processing of livestock. There are known former forges (one in the old brick building at the junction of Green Road and North Terrace), and there is some charming custom-made glasswork in one of the cottages on the south side of the High Street naming it as The Forge – not authenticated but perfectly possible.

The main source of income for the resident family at the castle was from the land, both what was grown and reared on it and what lay under it. The sloping land to the south of the High Street shows the scars of many years of stone quarrying, which preceded the discovery and exploitation of ironstone in the region, and of course the stone won from that ground is visible in many of the cottages in the village. The presence of local easily-extracted freestone will have encouraged development of the village, both because it meant employment and because houses were cheaper to build in a durable material available right there on the spot, with minimal transport costs.

We know from our archaeological investigations (see the Boroughgate section) that the first attempts to develop a village centre, under the direct influence of the owners of the castle, was on a north – south axis in the location known as Boroughgate, in line with the main entrance to the castle grounds. The dig at Boroughgate revealed an older, planned village on an alignment directed by a medieval landowner, but the village as it stands today is in a new orientation, at right angles to the planned layout. Skelton swung round 90 degrees as the village developed away from the taxed and ordered trading street laid out and overseen by the castle. Perhaps this reflects a decline of feudal control during the later Middle Ages. The village never seems to have developed much west of the castle. Possibly, the landowners were more willing to release land for dwellings on the hilly area to the south and east as this was harder to cultivate. They would wish to preserve the more desirable agricultural land westwards towards Skelton Ellers.

At some point in the Middle Ages the Boroughgate settlement withered away. It is hard to be sure whether there was an actual gap between the failure of Boroughgate and the inception of the village on its current axis, but that seems unlikely. There was agricultural work to be done. There was passing trade on the through routes, bringing travellers to be serviced. The new orientation was more conveniently situated on the level in the shelter of the contour along which the old part of the village stretches to this day. A southerly offshoot up Green Road, parallel to the defunct Boroughgate, climbs to where other routes from Guisborough and all points south, east, and west come in, at modern-day Skelton Green.

The road running northwards down towards Marske and the coast has, on its west side, some buildings of the early- to mid-19th century on castle estate land. These include estate worker dwellings of a superior sort, and a stone lean-to which serves the walled garden within the castle grounds. Within the lean-to was a now defunct furnace serving the magnificent walled gardens. Within those gardens, for example, is an arched brick cellar which was a temple for the cultivation of rhubarb; grown in the dark in earthen beds warmed by pipes leading from that furnace. By this means, the rhubarb could be available in the lean months of late winter and early spring when most fruits were not. These gardens, their vegetable beds, heated walls, and greenhouses, provided the castle residents and guests with vegetables and fruits, many of them exotic and hard to find until imports took over in the last third of the 20th century. In later times, the surplus would be sold off on summer Sundays to local customers. Older people still living in Skelton can remember queues of cars in Marske Lane filled with eager buyers. And hidden in the shed above the rhubarb cellar was found a stock of Skelton Castle carrier bags from those days. Collectors' items now!

Of course, shopping has shifted further along the street but the number and variety of thriving small to medium-sized shops is quite exceptional in these times when much larger settlements struggle to maintain a viable shopping centre. (See also 'Shopping in Victorian Skelton' section.) There's a 'right size' factor here, as with the continuity of building types. Skelton never outgrew its local community, so is not cluttered with redundant banks, department stores, and other over-large shops and institutional buildings, which have outlived their usefulness. This has helped the High Street to remain harmonious in style. It's a wide handsome space too, as the small shops without front gardens are set back to the frontage line of the residential properties to their west, yielding wide pavements which make shopping much more pleasant than in less fortunate neighbouring settlements whose narrower streets are oppressed by modern traffic.

The width of this street means Skelton is blessed with plenty of (currently free!) parking bays as well as wide pavements for shopping and socialising – it's rare to stroll along the stretch of pavement between the Pantry and the Wharton Arms without seeing several greetings and spontaneous conversations.

Moving eastwards along the High Street you can spot clues to economic change in the village. Around the Green and on the first stretch of the street, buildings are mostly stone or made of subtly shaded and textured handmade local brick.

Once the shops start, brick predominates as far as the Wharton Arms on the north side. The south side of the shopping area is dominated by the Co-op, a fine original building from the great age of Co-operative development above its modern street level frontage. Looking down from The Hills, you can see the old Cash Office projecting from the roof, in which current village residents can remember working.

At the end of this run of shops is a terrace which is built from machine-made red brick, more uniform in colour and shape than the subtly modulated shades and texture of the local brick dominating up to that point. This marks the date at which the railway came to Skelton (see the Railways section of this booklet), when cheaper transport made non-local building materials available in bulk. The railway came to the region relatively late, only after there was something valuable to convey out of the area, namely ironstone, which made it financially worthwhile to build lines. So, estate buildings of this boom period (the Wharton Arms and the terrace to its east) are all built in industrially manufactured red brick.

The railways were a by-product of the ironstone boom, as were the terraces of little two-up two-down cottages in Dixon Street and Yeoman Street. These were built to house the ironstone mine workers, as more and more men poured in from areas of the country where work was scarce or more poorly paid.

This is a familiar story (see the Social Impact section of this booklet) in which many local families have their roots. The new cottages are more uniform in pattern than the older, more organic, or piecemeal building which gradually grew the High Street eastwards and Green Road northwards. The new cottages had to be built in a hurry to meet a large-scale need.

However, looking at the rows of houses along Dixon Street (opposite), there is still variety – it's likely that the houses were built in batches as opportunity presented, probably by different small-scale firms or individual contractors who could pick up small parcels of land. Where later render has been removed, or at the rear of properties, older brick is visible; the machine-made product hadn't yet become readily available and cheap enough to take over for low-cost housing. Despite the haste and basic specifications, these cottages have stood the test of time and remain popular homes. So, those artisan builders did a decent job.

Public Houses and Places of Worship

Village life outside the home traditionally revolved around the church and the inn. Skelton is well served in both categories.

Two prominent buildings on the High Street, the Wharton Arms and All Saints Church, reflect the ironstone mining boom and the influx of both people and money that it brought. Local landowners were paid 'royalties' or a payment per ton of stone excavated from mines under their land. At the other end of the economic system, men were drawn, from areas of the country where jobs were fewer or earnings less, to swell the necessary workforce for the mines. These two buildings are a consequence of those changes.

First, the inn. On early Ordnance Survey maps (1856 edition), a Wharton Arms is shown in a different position from the present building, nearer to the older centre of the High Street.

When traffic and incomes increased, this was evidently deemed inadequate. A grand new establishment, called Hotel and not merely Public House, was built on a cleared site beyond the village centre, on the north side of the High Street. It was alongside the passing traffic and had a large yard behind to accommodate horses, carriages and stabling for them. Its frontage bears the date 1878, picked out in white bricks. Long-time Skelton residents remember fondly the sprung dance floor in the function room on the first floor of the west wing of the building. This was an important social centre for the village in quite recent times. Although the Wharton Arms still has its regulars, it is quite a different place from the dance hall years. Its new owner has renovated all the public rooms and the bedroom suites. A tearoom has been established in the east wing.

Looking at the building from across the road, you realise that it's not symmetrical. The west wing projects further and is wider than the east wing. The current entrance door is not central to the frontage.

The narrower east wing has an aged double door with above it an antique metal bracket, likely to have once supported an inn sign.

Running across the frontage is a decorative line of bull-nosed brick known as a 'string course' which turns the south-eastern corner.

But then it stops, on the side elevation, at exactly the depth of the eastern wing's projection from the rest of the building. Looking at this end wall you can also see that the window openings have brick infill below their sills, showing that they have been reduced in height from a door to a window. Why is this?

Well, further along the High Street, to the east, is a terrace of red-brick cottages. We'll discuss these in a moment.

For now, note that the width of the gap between the east gable of the Wharton Arms and the west gable of the cottages is exactly the same as the width of the façade of the Wharton Arms, minus its east wing. This, together with the truncated string-course, shows that the building was originally planned to have a further bay and wing beyond the current eastern end. It was intended to be a totally symmetrical building. This idea is also supported by the western gable end of the brick terrace being built with all stretchers (long sides of bricks facing). This pattern of bricks is unusual on an outside wall and more typical of a partition wall between conjoined buildings. Had the Wharton Arms been completed to the original, full design, the old door with the sign bracket above it would have been central.

The brick cottages were put up as housing for the families of Skelton Castle estate workers, and indeed the easternmost house was a pay office for the estate. The pay office window, with its brick arch leading to it, is currently protected from vandalism by the block-work wall at the north-eastern corner. Like the pub, these houses appear on maps in the late 19th century. They are definitely a 'cut above' many other terraces both in the high quality of the decorative brickwork lavished upon their frontage, and also the more fundamental amenity of having individual privies instead of a shared block, as much 19th century workers' housing did. These can still be seen, as pitched-roof outbuildings in the row of yards along the house backs.

One retains the door of the earth closet, a rare survival. The waste from the earth closet would be captured in a wooden box or zinc tub located behind the trapdoor. Once a week, the contents of the tub would be emptied by the night soil men, or 'gong-scourers'. This ancient term was still used locally until this practice died out with modern sewerage and plumbing. The night soil was carted away and most ended up spread on the land along with other small-scale domestic waste, hopefully after a spell of rotting down or composting. At the rear of this brick terrace was a large complex of buildings, Home Farm. These were demolished in recent times.

Careful examination of the detail of a building can tell a whole story of ambition and the rise and fall of fortunes. Perhaps the foregoing examples may give you a taste for detective work when walking the streets of your own neighbourhood!

Just a few yards east of Home Farm stands All Saints parish church. There was already a long-established church in Skelton, tucked down a lane on the fringes of the castle grounds. But in the second half of the 19th century, a grand, new edifice was put up, with substantial financial contributions from local landowners and businessmen.

One reason for the new building can be seen at the bottom of Green Road where a large and handsome former Methodist church stands. Another, smaller and earlier, former chapel stands on the other side of the same road.

There was yet another chapel, of the Primitive Methodists, further up Green Road so perhaps the Wesleyan mainstream also felt the need to compete with that.

The date of the later, grander chapel is 1877, one year earlier than that of the Wharton Arms. We can picture the near frenzy of building activity consuming Skelton in those years, driven by expanding congregations. It almost seems as though the chapel and church were stepping up to counterbalance the increase in tavern provision!

In the 19th century, nonconformist chapels were springing up all over the district to accommodate the growing population of workers associated with the mining boom. Many came from remote parts of the country such as Wales or Cornwall with strong chapel movements. Naturally the established, Anglican, church had to fight back, and the old church would not be sufficiently spacious to embrace the many potential worshippers – nor was its interior particularly welcoming to newcomers. Skelton is fortunate that the site of the old church was not deemed suitable for a much larger new building – it was nestled into the fringes of the castle grounds and, among other reasons, perhaps a larger, more urban church congregation wasn't an attractive prospect for the family at the castle. As a result, the old church remains intact instead of having been demolished and rebuilt, as happened in many other locations.

The two buildings are a fine contrast in style both internally and externally. Although the general brief of the Snapshot in Time was to focus on the exteriors of buildings, since these are both public places the interiors are available to anyone who wishes to see them so it seems fair enough to discuss them here.

The old church has medieval origins and traces can be seen outside the building at the chancel end. Anglo-Saxon burials have been found in the vicinity so we can assume that this has been a religious site for more than one thousand years. However, the church was almost entirely rebuilt in the 18th century in the plain classical style popular at that time. The interior is dominated by the pulpit, a rare surviving 'three-decker' with a desk below for the clerk. Partly under the influence of Methodism, and other preaching-driven nonconformist religions, the sermon became the centrepiece of the church service; ornamentation and ritual were out of fashion, being a distraction from focus on the Word.

There is also the evidence of regular use by a resident landowning family in the private pew with its personal fireplace, directly facing the pulpit; and the pews generally speak of an era when even church attendance was hierarchical, with the best seats often reserved for, or even rented by, the better-off families and 'free seats' for the poorer members of society at the rear of the building. The pews have doors with locks on them and some have dado panels bearing the names of the owning families. For example: the name Dixon appears on a front pew on the south side of the aisle. The Dixon family were still landowners in the area at the time of the development of Lingdale mine, where their holdings gave them a share of the royalties. There was an actual job of 'pew-opener' at many churches, often the perquisite of elderly widows of the parish. They would unlock pew doors to admit the owners, generally expecting a 'consideration' (a tip).

The gallery at the west end of the church and a few benches (the 'free seats') were the only spaces available for the servant and labouring classes to attend divine service. Maybe this exclusivity makes it even easier to see how Methodism and other nonconformist sects took hold in the village.

The new All Saints attracted generous funding and is lavish in detail inside and out, with the exceptionally unusual feature of a detached bell tower. Inside it shows the influence of 19th century religious thought such as the Oxford movement which sought to restore the mystical element to church services, with a darker, more numinous and heavily ornamented interior and a chancel separated from the nave where the congregation sat, so that the priest was seen more at a distance and as a celebrant rather than primarily a preacher. At the same time there is much more generous, open access seating making all classes more welcome. Meanwhile, the Green Road Methodist church of 1877 mentioned above was also highly decorated and colourful - and further up Green Road can be seen an example of the reaction against this trend in Methodism, a former Primitive Methodist chapel, pretty but more austere, its style and restraint felt by its adherents to reflect the original vision of John Wesley. So, Skelton's religious buildings illustrate prevailing theological trends from the 18th to the 20th century.

One curious feature in such a large village is that there is no Roman Catholic church, whereas Brotton, the much smaller neighbouring settlement, does have one.

Both Anglican churches shared the fine large Rectory, now a private house. This was erected in 1817, replacing a two-storey thatched predecessor. It was further extended in 1857.

Beyond the Mosaic Trail

Once the Mosaic Trail gets you interested in the life of buildings, here are a few suggestions to seek out either while walking that trail or on expeditions of your own around the streets of Skelton:

What do you think about numbers 61 and 63? Can you see that they used to be one long building, as the stone joints run right across and the two fronts doors are later inserts? They are handsome dwellings now but would have been a single, very substantial, building of classic 'longhouse' form when built, They are likely to date back to the 18th century. The size and elevated position suggest it may have been a late medieval yeoman property.

Numbers 29/31 High Street are now known as Sundial House, which does bear a fine sundial dated 1787. However, it's unsafe to date a building by such an ornament. It isn't built into the wall but supported on a bracket. A valuable item like this would have been rescued if its original location were demolished. The house itself is a handsome one and, despite the cautionary words, is in period for the date shown.

Have a look at the door frame of Hauxwell House, number 27, which shows the same elegant and elaborate panelling to the interior as survives in a few of the shops further down the street such as Coral Bookmakers and the optician's at 107.

Its adjoining property has fine decorative brickwork on its front face, with stone quoins (corner-stones); look round to the side elevation, which shows the underlying build to be stone; this illustrates the relative prestige of stone and brick at the time, when brick was hand-made and more costly. (You can see the exact opposite in the new builds on the opposite side of the street, which have been fronted in stone but are brick-clad behind).

Further along, the optician's, at 107, retains, as well as its fine doorcase - needing some love and care but intact - its little flight of steps with an elegant curving handrail, a charming as well as useful feature.

Looking up to The Hills, you can see both fine Victorian villas and 20th century bay-windowed bungalows. These are built on old quarry land, set into the hillside on a terrace along the ancient route of Swilly Lane, and they mark the time when householders really began to appreciate the scenic value of the region, its hills and sea views. Those handsome villas were built in an era of horse transport and were probably always pretty tricky to reach in adverse weather – but they're worth it for the magnificent view, which is a luxury consideration over and above considerations of mere convenience. These house sites were chosen for pleasure, which shows a new level of prosperity when consumer choices became more widely available in society. It also suggests that Skelton, and the region's villages generally, were becoming desirable places to live, not just somewhere you ended up in your search to make a home. Perhaps, also, should be factored in that the High Street was becoming increasingly busy with traffic.

Those villas would have been quite exciting and novel when built in the 19th century. Another example of a new build challenging local expectations is down Marske Lane. 'Nimrod' was architect-designed to make the most of its plot space, and to catch the views. Opinions of it may differ but it is innovative and shows commitment to a tricky site.

Also on the south side of the High Street, at the eastern end, is Eggcup Farm. What we can see from the road appears to be a plain 19th century farmhouse, but there is rubble walling to the interior and outbuildings which may suggest a much earlier build date. It is popularly believed to be one of the oldest buildings remaining in the village. However, it is notoriously hard to date traditional buildings in local materials.

And on that theme, returning to the north side of the High Street, to the east of the church there are two suggestive groups of buildings. The first is Robinson Street, where some of the houses at the top end (particularly 2 to 4) have indications of earlier masonry, especially at ground floor level, as do the garden walls opposite, and the suggestion of those recording this terrace was that these houses pre-dated the others in the street and may date from the 17th century. Look for yourself and see what you think.

Further along the High Street, numbers 153 and 155 are also especially fascinating and suggest many eras of occupation for different purposes. We know for a fact that 155, which is 18th or early 19th century in origin, spent the 1960s and early 70s as a Gas Board showroom, but it's survived to form a handsome dwelling. Number 153, adjoining to the west, is even more complex. The masonry on the front appears to show three levels of different stonework, from massive, rough-hewn blocks at the base of the wall through two levels of better dressed, coursed stone to the roof. Old photographs show that the first-floor windows were the traditional wide and shallow shape which accommodated traditional Yorkshire casements, with sideways sliding panes. This shape has been retained in the modern replacements. The current imposing door is more or less central, but immediately to its left (facing the building) is a window with clear indications that it was once a door – infill masonry below and traces of a step and lintel; and even more suggestive, deeply incised stones to its sides created by being used to sharpen tools over a period of many years. The building is thought to have been a grain store in the 19th and early 20th century, but the sharpening stones imply some other use: it may have been an early longhouse whose inhabitants routinely honed their implements on leaving or returning. The rough-grained local sandstone serves this purpose admirably for ordinary tools; no need to waste time and trouble on seeking out and using a whetstone. These grooves put us within touching distance of the daily life and work of Skelton men of the past who may have no other memorial but have left their mark here in the stones of an ordinary wall. I think that's pretty exciting!

You're probably getting the idea of 'reading a building' if it was new to you, so now to throw in a curve ball on how one can get tripped up on dating. There are many charming stone cottages along Green Road but if you make the uphill trip, you'll find a sweet little terrace on the right just before Wiltshire Road. The topmost of these cottages (no.24) looks a little grander than the others. It has a gable with various ornaments, and some fascinating carved stonework built into the walls here and there. It's so tempting to start thinking lovely medieval thoughts, especially as the end, gable, wall is of rubble construction, so the building is likely to be genuinely quite old.

However, the antique carved details seem a little random, not consistent in date and rather oddly placed on a dwelling house. It turns out that either the current or previous owners, when renovating the property, were more creative and innovative than usual and sourced various interesting relics from salvage yards or demolitions of older buildings. The effect is charmingly eclectic but illustrates how easy it is to be misled by alterations!

Summary

Buildings recording forces us to look – really look – at the frontage of a property from top to bottom; and also at the sides and rear of a building where we can. This often reveals concealed information about the structure and its previous use and form. Skelton is a particularly rewarding site for this activity. In the older part of the village there is little formal planned building, nor tracts of uniform housing; hardly even a run of terraced housing until miners' cottages start to appear around the edges of the village in the late 19th century.

Where terraces appear, close examination often reveals that not all were put up as a single run of dwellings. Study the roof lines, the window alignments, and the masonry and you'll see a history of infill and change of use. In other locations, owners have enterprisingly extended, sideways, upwards, and backwards, sometimes reusing some rather exotic pieces of stone garnered from even older buildings (see No 24 Green Road mentioned above).

Deciphering the complex stories of these homes can be tricky but all have stories, stories of their human inhabitants and their lives and changing needs. It is also a story of survival; quite humble buildings have been 'pre-loved' and kept alive by being adapted by the current inhabitants as the village itself has grown and changed with each generation.

The more conspicuous public buildings tell the formal social history of the village's development. Chapels were added to accommodate new beliefs or more residents – most now deconsecrated and converted for other uses. A new, bigger Anglican church was erected to keep up traditional faith in the face of the growth in Nonconformism. Schools were built in which to educate the young folk, some being built and demolished within a single lifetime.

The building materials used illustrate the social history of the village. Quite modest homes in the area are stone-built. This came about partly because brick manufacture was slow to take off in the era. Therefore, bricks were in scarce supply before the railways allowed easy import of materials manufactured elsewhere. Even before the ironstone era, there was extensive quarrying for building stone in Skelton itself and the bumpy hillsides to the south of the High Street are a reminder of this former industry. It's this predominance of local materials that gives the built environment in Skelton its homely and harmonious feel.

Other examples of cultural change are the fine houses built up on the elevated ground at The Hills. The main village developed along the contour, nestled into the shelter of the hillside along a conveniently level track which became the High Street and in due course the main road to Whitby; the attraction seems obvious by comparison with the steep gradient along which Boroughgate was positioned.

The Victorian boom years permitted more luxurious choices: larger, showier dwellings for the first time, sited to take advantage of the newly desirable sea views; followed in the 20th century by picture-window bungalows. Both styles of dwelling were made possible by improvements in glass manufacture permitting larger and larger panes.

Skelton's had its ups and downs over the centuries, as has its resident landowning family at the castle, but both have shown flexibility and resilience in the face of changing conditions and with the injection of funds and volunteer energies pumping new life into the High Street, it now presents a thriving face to the world. With a wide range of good housing stock, a beautiful location, excellent transport links and unusually good shopping and eating out opportunities, it's a lively and vital village with a strong sense of local identity.

If you live in Skelton and your house isn't mentioned, that doesn't mean it's not full of interest, just that this isn't a catalogue. The results of Snapshot in Time have been stored at Teesside Archives, where they are accessible, on request, by any member of the public.

There is still plenty to be discovered and if you notice something interesting or know something about the history and background to Skelton, the Skelton History Group would love to hear from you. Our web presence can be found at *skeltonhistorygroup.org.uk*. Please use the Contact tab on the website to ask questions or provide information.

The Mosaic Trail

Howard Wilson

The Skelton Townscape Heritage project consisted of improvements to the High Street and some associated activities. These latter were intended to engage the community with the village`s history and heritage. One such activity was the creation of a Mosaic Trail. The major conditions of the Heritage Lottery funded grant for the mosaics (£250 each) was that they would complement the existing mosaics which were installed as part of an earlier initiative and reflect the heritage of the property on which they were installed.

The area of focus was between the 'old' and 'new' churches in Skelton to take in a route along the High Street. Also included was Boroughgate Lane, as another significant location. Its inclusion linked the Trail with the archaeological investigation of the village's medieval origins. One of the mosaics was incorporated into one of the interpretation panels at Boroughgate.

The Trail, which was specifically supported by our partner, the Skelton & Brotton Parish Council, had an ambitious aim: to develop 27 small mosaic panels to be installed along the length of the village's main street, from All Saints parish church in the east to old All Saints church in the west. The chosen properties are tabulated at the end of this chapter.

Jo Mead, the Community Development Officer for Skelton, Brotton and Loftus Wards, also a member of the Skelton Townscape Heritage board, was the project lead, reporting progress back to the monthly board meetings and updating the Project Manager.

Skelton High Street, from church to church
Contains Ordnance Survey data – Crown Copyright

The old church is in the top left corner, and the parish church is at the top right.

The activity was broken down into two phases, running over two years. Phase 1 included 13 mosaics, the remaining 14 were produced during phase 2. For each property, the basic research was carried out by the Community Development Officer and Skelton History Group, using census returns, business directories, and internet searches to identify those buildings with interesting histories in their own right, or interesting occupations of those who lived there. The time-period of primary interest was the Victorian era. However, if an earlier or later period offered useful ideas, these were given consideration.

Of all the research processes, the interrogation of the census returns proved the most useful, if time consuming. It involved starting at one end of the High Street and listing every property and owner`s occupation.

Numerous locations were identified, and residents and owners were visited or contacted to ascertain their interest in having a mosaic installed on the property that would reflect its history.

Once agreement was in place, an information pack was created for each property. In phase 2, several of the owners who had initially been interested no longer desired to be involved necessitating new property searches. The overall objectives were to have the mosaics spread out along the route, with no clusters, and no duplication of occupations.

Workshops then took place with Freebrough Academy art students, the Community Artists (Helen Gaunt and Derek Mosey) contracted to create the mosaics, and the Community Development Officer. The students used the information packs and carried out their own research to develop a series of design ideas. These were then turned into outline designs and from those were produced the final mosaics.

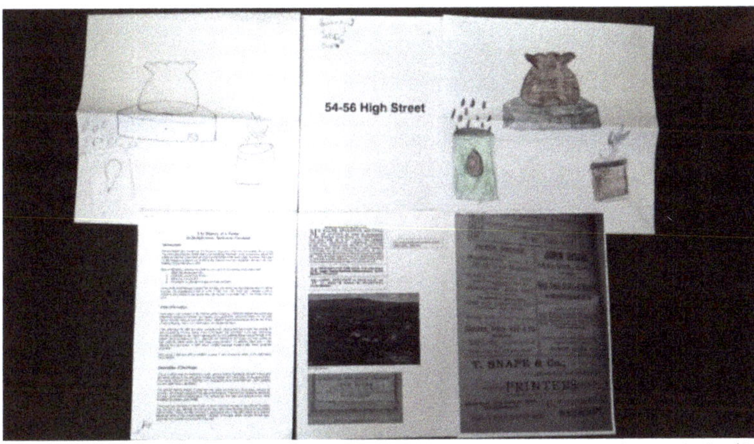

An information pack (above bottom) and the students' design ideas (above top) for 54-56 High Street

Outline design

Final mosaic

The mosaic for the old Rectory followed the same basic process. However, this time, during an internet search we were fortunate to come across this photograph of the Reverend Drake who was Vicar of All Saints from June 1911 to 1920.

(Photo courtesy of skeltonincleveland.com website)

Herbert Mackworth Drake was born in June 1870 at Veryan in Cornwall; the first son of Charles Mackworth and Georgina Drake. In 1881, aged 10 he was a boarder at "The Grammar School" at St Clement, Cornwall. By 1891 he was a student at Oxford. He became Vicar of All Saints in June 1911 – leaving in 1920.

He married Mary Margaret Slater on the 21st of July 1903 at the Parish Church of Bideford in the County of Devon and was a well-travelled man, visiting Tenerife four times between 1906 and 1934. He apparently travelled alone as no trace of his wife or children could be found on the ship's passenger lists.

To find a photograph of a Skelton Vicar who was in residence during our time-period was, indeed, very fortuitous so it was decided to design a mosaic based on his portrait.

(above right) the outline design,
(left) the completed mosaic

Once the outline designs for the mosaics were completed, the Community Development Officer liaised with the property owners to gain their approval. Occasionally, more than one design was submitted, and the final choice was left up to the property owners. Any requested amendments were carried out and resubmitted for final approval. The final design was then transferred by the artists to a mosaic board.

To fulfil the Heritage Lottery Funds requirement of "engaging the community with the village's history and heritage" the Community Development Officer then liaised with local community groups, educational establishments and venues within Skelton to facilitate workshops where members of the public and school children could contribute to the creation of the finished mosaics. Workshops were held at Skelton Library and Civic Hall, De Brus Youth Centre, and Skelton Primary School. Freebrough Academy art students were also given the opportunity to create mosaics they had helped to design.

On completion of the mosaics the Community Development Officer, and the mosaic artists, visited each property and agreed the location of the mosaics with the owners.

To facilitate this process, "mock-up" images were created – see example to the left of No. 37 High St – Shoemaker.

Both phase 1 and phase 2 included at least one listed building. For each of these, "Listed Building Consent" was needed before the mosaic could installed. With the consent of the property owners, the Community Development Officer prepared and submitted the necessary planning applications to Redcar and Cleveland Borough Council, each of which was subsequently approved.

At the completion of phase 1, an interim "Mosaic Trail" leaflet was produced by Skelton History Group which included images of the mosaics in situ and a brief description of the property research information. Upon completion of phase 2, a new leaflet was produced which included all the mosaics from both phases, plus the six mosaics from the previous project.

The total community volunteer time for research, owner visits, design, and creation of the 27 mosaics, over the two phases, was just over 700 hours.

The archaeological excavations of Boroughgate Lane took place after the completion of the phase 2 work with community groups, so the design of this mosaic was based on finds from the excavation. The mosaic was assembled by members of the public at the medieval re-enactment event in August 2018, which was another activity within the heritage project. A separate information leaflet was produced about the history of Boroughgate and the finds and knowledge that came out of the archaeological investigation.

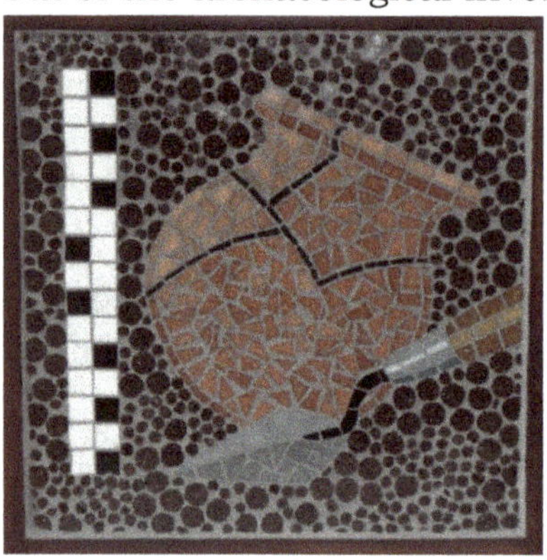

Pot & trowel mosaic

Pot “in situ”

Acknowledgements

Special thanks are due to:

Jo Mead, Community Development Officer, for leading this activity.

Pam Batts, Skelton Villages Civic Pride, for knocking on doors to canvass support from property owners.

Community Artists, Helen Gaunt and Derek Mosey, for turning the students' design ideas into the finished mosaics.

Residents and children of Skelton, and Freebrough Academy art students, for helping to create the mosaics.

Property owners, for their support and agreement to have mosaics installed on their properties.

Properties and their mosaics

Phase 1

Address	***Mosaic depicting***
7 North Terrace	Wood Sawyer
1-3 The Old School	Infants School
4 South Terrace	Boer War Hospital
9 South Terrace, York House	Doctors Surgery
The Old Rectory	Skelton Vicar 1911-1920
54-56 High Street	Seed Merchant
Skelton Fire Station	Smithy
Skelton Community Orchard	Market Garden
85 High Street	Jeweller & Watch Repairer
98 High Street	Milliner & Volunteer WW1 Nurse
101 High Street	Plumbers
106 High Street	Forester
145 High Street	Estate Pay Booth

Phase 2

Address	***Mosaic depicting***
Boroughgate	Medieval Village
Old All Saints Church	Closed Church
9 North Terrace, Royal George	Coaching Inn
14 North Terrace	Gas House
1 South Terrace	Police Station
23 High Street	School Science Teacher
24 High Street Sterne Cottages	Sledging Field to the Rear
37 High Street	Shoemaker
40 High Street	Ironstone Worker
67 High Street	Church Organist
72 High Street	Chemist
89 High Street	Painter & Paper Hanger
115 High Street	Mine Engineman
120 High Street, Lien House	Iron Moulder

Railways around Skelton & East Cleveland

Geoffrey Allen

Early Proposals

Prior to the railway age, the only ways for people to move around the area were Shank's Pony (i.e. on foot), riding a horse, or travelling in a horse-drawn vehicle. For bulky goods and minerals, it was generally considered that the most efficient means of moving these was a canal, a solution unsuited to our local topography.

With the discovery of ironstone in the East Cleveland area, thoughts quickly turned to how to get it from the mines to the ironworks. A typical horse drawn wagon pulled by a single horse on the roads of the day could only manage 2 tons at best. A canal boat drawn by the same horse could manage about 50 tons in theory but, because of the narrow boats in use, probably no more than about 25 tons.

It quickly became clear that railways were the main answer to the transport problems. Although, it should be noted that in the early days of the industry, some ironstone was exported by small ships from the foreshore at Skinningrove and other places, plus the harbour at Whitby. The first railway to approach the Skelton area was the erstwhile Middlesbrough & Guisborough Railway which opened for business in 1854.

The map (overleaf) shows the main mines in the immediate vicinity of Skelton. Please note that all the mines shown would not have been in operation at the same time. Indeed, several mines, for example, Kilton (1875 to 1897) & Longacres (1915 to 1935), spent considerable periods 'mothballed'.

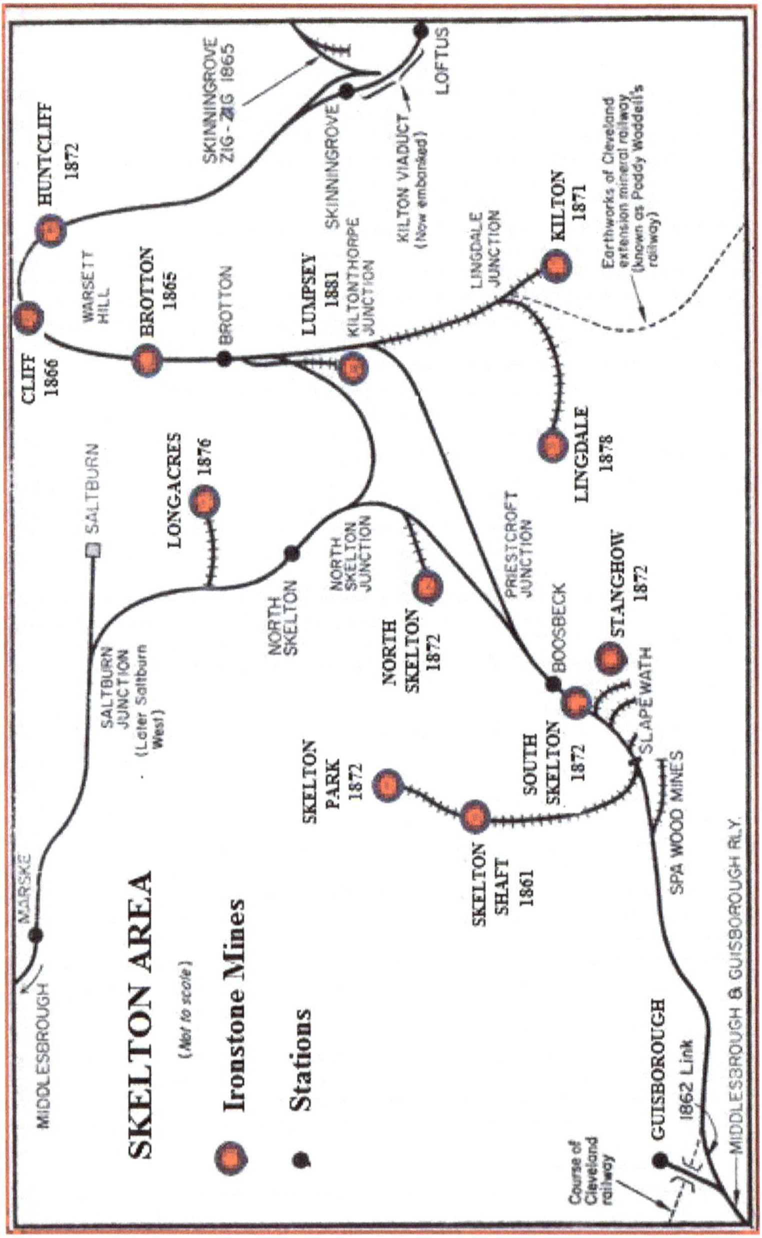
SKELTON AREA
(Not to scale)
Ironstone Mines
Stations
MIDDLESBROUGH
MARSKE
SALTBURN
SALTBURN JUNCTION (Later Saltburn West)
LONGACRES 1876
NORTH SKELTON
NORTH SKELTON JUNCTION
NORTH SKELTON 1872
CLIFF 1866
WARSETT HILL
BROTTON 1865
BROTTON
HUNTCLIFF 1872
SKINNINGROVE ZIG-ZAG 1865
SKINNINGROVE
LOFTUS
KILTON VIADUCT (Now embanked)
LUMPSEY 1881
KILTONTHORPE JUNCTION
LINGDALE JUNCTION
KILTON 1871
Earthworks of Cleveland extension mineral railway (known as Paddy Waddell's railway)
LINGDALE 1878
PRIESTCROFT JUNCTION
BOOSBECK
STANGHOW 1872
SLAPEWATH
SOUTH SKELTON 1872
SPA WOOD MINES
SKELTON PARK 1872
SKELTON SHAFT 1861
GUISBOROUGH
1862 Link
Course of Cleveland railway
MIDDLESBROUGH & GUISBOROUGH RLY.
MIDDLESBROUGH

Railway Opening dates

Middlesbrough & Guisborough Railway

- Opened to goods traffic: 11th November 1853
- Opened to passenger traffic: 25th February 1854

Stockton & Darlington Railway

- Redcar Junction to Saltburn, opened to goods and passenger traffic: 17th August 1861

Cleveland Railway

- Cargo Fleet Jetty to Slapewath, opened 23rd November 1861 (closed from Normanby to Guisborough in 1865)
- Slapewath to Skelton Shaft Mine, opened 23rd November 1861
- Slapewath to Boosbeck, opened for goods traffic in1862 and for passenger traffic on 1st November 1878
- Boosbeck to Brotton, opened for goods traffic on 23rd February 1865 and for passenger traffic on 1st November 1878
- Brotton to Skinningrove, opened for goods traffic on 21st April 1865 and for passenger traffic on 1st April 1875

North Eastern Railway

- Saltburn West Junction to Brotton via North Skelton, opened for goods traffic on 1st June 1872 and for passenger traffic on 1st April 1875
- Skelton Shaft Mine to Skelton Park Mine, opened in 1872 (for goods traffic only)
- North Skelton Junction to Priestcroft Junction, opened in January 1873
- Lingdale Junction to Lingdale, opened in 1878 (for goods traffic only)

Private Railway (J.T. Wharton)

- Kiltonthorpe Junction to Kilton Mine, opened in 1871 (for goods traffic only)

The first mention of a railway in the Skelton area appears in Tomlinson's 'North Eastern Railway'. It is recorded that a parliamentary bill for this railway was first proposed in 1858. That bill was defeated three times due to determined opposition from the Saltburn & Darlington Railway. A new parliamentary bill, for what would eventually become the Cleveland Railway, was prepared in 1860/61. This time it was passed subject to *'stringent provisions for safeguarding the rights of the Tees Conservancy Commissioners and to ensure the completion of the line to Skinningrove'* (Tomlinson, p.575). Included in this act was a branch line to 'Skelton New Mine' (which would become Skelton Shaft), which opened for business in 1861. By 1872 The Skelton Shaft branch had been extended to reach Skelton Park.

Returning once more to the 1858 Parliamentary session, this contained a bill from the Stockton & Darlington *'authorising them to extend their Redcar line to Saltburn and Skelton'* (Tomlinson, p.568). This extract does not specify what was meant by Skelton. Indeed, it would be 1872 before such a line from Saltburn would be driven across the Skelton Beck on a monumental viaduct, to reach the Skelton area from the north.

In the meantime, the Cleveland Railway had reached Boosbeck by 1862, and Brotton and Skinningrove by 1865. In 1872 the aforementioned Saltburn Extension was opened by the North Eastern Railway. At first it was for goods traffic only, as were all the local lines east of Guisborough. The North Eastern took over the private railway to Kilton Mine in 1874 and built the Lingdale branch in 1878. The short branches to North Skelton and Stanghow pits opened in 1872 and to Longacres in 1876, which essentially completed the East Cleveland network. Of interest is that whilst under construction North Skelton pit was served by a temporary branch line from the Cleveland Railway near where it crossed Stanghow Lane, the line passing Wet Furrows farm on its way to the site.

As stated earlier the railways of East Cleveland were primarily laid to transport ironstone from the mines to the steelworks on Tees-side, at Skinningrove and in county Durham. The North Eastern Railway probably viewed the provision of a passenger service as something they might have to do if forced but which interfered with the main reason for their existence. Be that as it may, from April 1st, 1875 the Saltburn Extension was opened to passenger traffic when the stations at Brotton, Skinningrove and Loftus opened. Boosbeck had to wait a little longer, until November 1st, 1878, for its station. However, the Skelton villages continued to be denied a station of their own. This lack of a station was to have tragic consequences for one man as this newspaper report, extracted from *History of Skelton* website, shows:

7th February 1881, Railway Fatality at North Skelton Junction

> *A melancholy accident happened on the railway at North Skelton on Saturday night. An old man [he was aged 65] named Zachariah Wilson, a joiner employed at the North Skelton mines, had been to Middlesbrough and had come back by train to Saltburn. Instead of coming back from Saltburn to his home at North Skelton by the turnpike road, he had gone part of the way on the line. He had got to the junction at North Skelton where he was met by the excursion train from Middlesbrough. His foot was taken off by the ankle and legs otherwise mutilated. He died this morning from the injuries received. He was found on the line by PC Calvert and his own son-in-law, Robert Bean.*

The lack of a station at Skelton meant that people had, by necessity, to travel by other means, usually by walking since few could afford a horse or carriage. For Skelton's residents to catch the train, meant a walk of approximately two miles to

Saltburn (station opened in 1861), Brotton (1875) or Boosbeck (1878) or 4½ miles to Guisborough (opened 1854).

To illustrate the pre-railway situation, from the 15th of June 1814 a stagecoach ran the approximately 35 miles from Whitby to Stockton (via Skelton & Redcar) at a cost of 14/- for outside passengers and 20/- for inside. This equates to 5d per mile in old money (outside) and 6½d (inside). Unfortunately, my source does not say how long this took! However, that said, most people would not have considered having to walk to a destination an unusual state of affairs; many people would walk further than this everyday just to get to and from work.

There continued to be a lively debate in Skelton about the denial, by the North Eastern Railway, of their wish for a station of their own and several letters survive to show progress, or lack of it, in this regard. A correspondent to Home Words for Heart & Hearth, Skelton Magazine 1895 wrote: *"By the way, the Skelton Railway Station is still the subject of words and promises rather than actions. Is the Railway Company putting off with the idea of making a light railway right up to our old market place?"*

How a light railway, as suggested above, could have been built is hard to understand. By their very nature light railways were a means of providing a service where a normal heavy railway could not be justified financially. Light railways were built on the cheap, with poorer track, minimal safety standards and signalling, and with fewer less well built structures and stations. In order to drive a railway from Guisborough to Saltburn, apart from difficult topography, meant that the existing terminus at Guisborough would need to be converted into a through station which was a major obstacle as the main local land owner was not exactly keen on the idea.

Undeterred, the local populace continued to press the North Eastern Railway for a station. As shown by a further quote from Home Words for Heart & Hearth, this time from 1898.

"However, all the doubters may pluck up heart again, and the prophets expect to see their prophecies exploded in the course of a month or two. A letter has been received within the last few days from Sir Joseph Pease, Chairman of the North-Eastern Railway Board of Directors, stating that all is ready, waiting for the Solicitor of the Company to complete the necessary documents for the conveyance of the land on which the station is to be built from Mr. Wharton to the Company. Mr. Gibb, the General Manager of the Company, is equally explicit that the station shall be erected. So, if promises mean anything, and they are in writing, leaving now no more latitude for misunderstanding, we shall have our station and that shortly."

Finally, in 1902, the Skelton villages got their station!

"Skelton Railway Station, the long-talked of railway station at Skelton is now an accomplished fact, having been quietly opened for passenger and goods traffic on Tuesday, July 1st. Standing as it does on two lines, the Saltburn and Scarborough Branch and the Saltburn and Guisborough Branch, it gives an excellent service of trains, no less than twelve each way, stopping to set down and take up passengers. This arrangement of trains seems likely to be both useful and convenient to us who live at Skelton or North or New Skelton, especially to and from Saltburn and Middlesbrough. The buildings though plain in appearance, inexpensive and simple in construction, are well adapted to our present requirements. The oil lamps are somewhat primitive and remind one of the dark ages, but they no doubt will give place to something more cheerful when our urban

Council has completed its plans with regard to Holly Bush Lane and the lighting thereof. Perhaps it is premature to expect the North Eastern to give us a free delivery of goods and parcels, as it does at Brotton, although Brotton has not a much greater population than Skelton now that has lost Boosbeck and the South side of the old parish. No doubt that and other things will come in time. Meanwhile we are very glad to have the station and find it very useful."

(Quote taken from *Home Words for Heart & Hearth*, Skelton & Boosbeck Magazine,1902)

The station, of mainly wooden construction, cost £1447 to build and is not unlike similar structures in the coal mining areas of County Durham. Although relatively cheap to construct this type of structure is ideal for areas where subsidence due to mineral extraction was likely to occur. There was a footbridge at the Saltburn end and the signal box was at the Brotton end on the down line. A substantial goods shed was also provided.

Although undated, the accompanying photographs (above and opposite) from the Ken Hoole Collection at Darlington show the station and signalling essentially intact, although as both sets of signals are cleared this suggests that the signal box was locked out and not manned when the photo was taken. In addition, the down-side waiting shelter appears to have been removed. The goods shed can be glimpsed behind the signal on the left-hand side. All of this suggests a date just prior or just after closure on the 8th of September 1951. The second view is also undated and from the same source but may have been taken about the same time as there are further signs of dereliction on the station platform but the platform lamps are still intact, so it is possibly just after closure. The engine is an A8 4-6-2T number 69893 on a Summer season Whitby to Middlesbrough service. Allocation records show that this engine was based at West Hartlepool until the 15th of September 1957. Additionally, the line from Brotton to Saltburn via North Skelton was closed to all passenger traffic from the 9th of September 1957, so it cannot be after that date. Of interest is the use of old sleepers to form the station platforms more evidence of the original need to build the station as cheaply as possible.

Below are the timetables for the Saltburn, Guisborough and Middlesbrough Autotrain services in 1910.

SALTBURN, GUISBOROUGH, and MIDDLESBROUGH (Auto-cars).

Up.	Week Days.													
	mrn	mrn	mrn	mrn	mrn	aft	aft (Sats. only.)	aft	aft	aft	aft	aft (Weds. and Sats.)		
Saltburn ....dep.	....	6 40	8 4	9 3	1121	1255	....	....	4 20	....	6 21	....	....	....
North Skelton	....	6 51	8 15	9 14	1131	1 6	....	....	4 30	....	6 31	....	....	....
Brotton .... arr.	....	6 55	....	9 18	1135	....	....	....	4 35	....	....	....	....	....
Brotton .... dep.	....	6 58	....	9 22	1138	....	2 30	....	4 38	....	....	....	....	....
Boosbeck	....	7 5	8 21	9 29	1145	1 12	2 37	....	4 45	....	6 37	....	....	....
Guisborough .... arr.	....	7 15	8 33	9 39	1155	1 22	2 47	....	4 55	....	6 46	....	....	....
Guisborough .... dep.	5 17	7 23	8 37	9 42	12 1	1 24		3 23	5 1	6 0	6 48	10 8	....	....
Hutton Gate	5 21	7 27	8 41	9 46	12 5	1 28		3 27	5 5	6 4	6 52	1012	....	....
Pinchingthorpe	5 25	7 31	8 45	9 50	12 9	1 32		3 31	5 9	6 8	6 56	1016	....	....
Nunthorpe 719	5 31	7 37	8 51	9 56	1215	1 38		3 37	5 15	6 14	7 2	1022	....	....
Ormesby	5 35	7 41	8 55	10 0	1219	1 42		3 41	5 19	6 18	7 6	1026	....	....
Middlesbrough *(see above)* ar	5 42	7 48	9 2	10 7	1226	1 49		3 48	5 26	6 25	7 13	1033	....	....

MIDDLESBROUGH, GUISBOROUGH, and SALTBURN (Auto-cars).

Miles.	Down.	Week Days.													
		mrn	mrn	mrn	mrn	aft	aft (Sats. only.)	aft	aft	aft	aft	aft	aft	aft (Weds. and Sats.)	
	Middlesbrough ....dep.	6 20	8 40	9 42	1157	1251		2 47	4 52	5 17	6 0	8 20	....	1048	....
3	Ormesby	6 27	8 47	9 49	12 4	1258		2 54	4 59	5 24	6 7	8 27	....	1055	....
4½	Nunthorpe	6 33	8 53	9 55	1210	1 4		3 0	5 5	5 30	6 13	8 33	....	11 1	....
7¼	Pinchingthorpe	6 39	8 59	10 1	1216	1 10		3 6	5 11	5 36	6 19	8 39	....	11 7	....
8¾	Hutton Gate	6 43	9 3	10 5	1220	1 14		3 10	5 15	5 40	6 23	8 43	....	1111	....
10	Guisborough .... arr.	6 47	9 7	10 9	1224	1 18		3 14	5 19	5 44	6.27	8 47	....	1115	....
	Guisborough .... dep.	6 49	9 10	1011	1226	....	1 45	3 16	5 21	....	....	....	8 54	....	....
14	Boosbeck	6 59	9 20	1021	1236	....	1 55	3 26	5 31	....	....	....	9 7	....	....
16¾	Brotton 718 .... arr.	7 4	9 26	....	....	....	2 0	3 31	5 36	....	....	....	9 12	....	....
	Brotton 718 .... dep.	....	....	....	....	....	....	3 37	5 42	....	....	....	9 18	....	....
18¼	North Skelton	....	....	1026	....	....	....	3 41	5 46	....	....	....	9 22	....	....
21	**Saltburn 707** ....arr.	....	....	1038	1247	....	....	3 53	5 58	....	....	....	9 35	....	....

Both extracts are from the Mike Hitches Collection in his book *Steam Around Middlesbrough.*

Autotrain working was an idea used by the North Eastern Railway to provide a cheap passenger service. In this arrangement, the locomotive was sandwiched between two or three coaches, the outermost of which were specially modified so the engine driver, through communication with the fireman on the footplate, could drive the train from either end. The driver however was the only one in control of the brakes. Communication between the two was by means of telegraphic code. This reduced time lost by the need for the train engine to run round its train at termini (such as Guisborough) and reversing points (in this case Brotton & Saltburn West Junction). By reference to the timetable above, you can see that, for the 10:11am Guisborough to Saltburn, reversals would have been needed at Guisborough, Hutton Junction and finally Saltburn West with arrival at Saltburn at 10:38, 27 minutes after leaving Guisborough. As this train did not call at Brotton it must have used the Priestcroft curve. For a train that called additionally at Brotton, such as the 3:16pm service, the journey time was ten minutes longer (37 minutes) arriving at Saltburn at 3:53pm. Such an Autotrain is seen below at Guisborough in the early 1900's.

© Gazette Live

The last of the North Eastern Railway BTP Class 0-4-4T engines was used on these trains, number 1436 of Guisborough shed, built by Hawthorn & Co. Newcastle in October 1875. It would have regularly visited North Skelton up to its withdrawal from service on the 23rd of November 1929 at the ripe old age of 54 Years! With 1436's withdrawal Class F8 2-4-2T number 685 took over. In November 1930 this was in turn replaced by 12 cylinder Sentinel railcar 'Old Blue', which lasted until 1941 when it, too, was replaced (on the 15th of September 1941) by G5 0-4-4T 1883. This engine remained at Guisborough (as 67281) until the shed closed on 20th September 1954, three years after passenger services from North Skelton had been finally withdrawn.

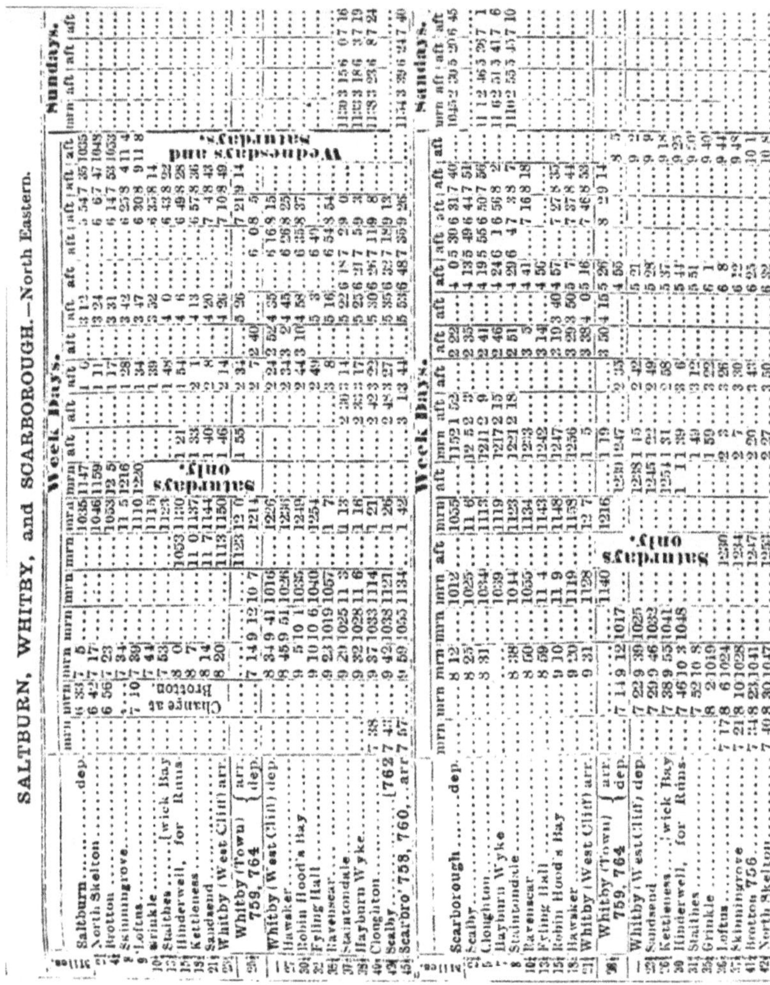

SALTBURN, WHITBY, and SCARBOROUGH.—North Eastern.

Week Days. | Sundays.

Saltburn dep.
North Skelton
Brotton
Skinningrove
Loftus
Grinkle
Staithes
Hinderwell, for Runswick Bay
Kettleness
Sandsend
Whitby (West Cliff) arr.
Whitby (Town) 759, 764 arr. / dep.
Whitby (West Cliff) dep.
Hawsker
Robin Hood's Bay
Fyling Hall
Ravenscar
Staintondale
Hayburn Wyke
Cloughton
Scalby
Scarbro' 758, 760, arr.

Week Days. | Sundays.

Scarborough dep.
Scalby
Cloughton
Hayburn Wyke
Staintondale
Ravenscar
Fyling Hall
Robin Hood's Bay
Hawsker
Whitby (West Cliff) arr.
Whitby (Town) 759, 764 arr. / dep.
Whitby (West Cliff) dep.
Sandsend
Kettleness
Hinderwell, for Runswick Bay
Staithes
Grinkle
Loftus
Skinningrove
Brotton 756
North Skelton
Saltburn 757 arr.

Other services that called at North Skelton, are illustrated by the extract from Bradshaw's directory of July 1926 (above). At this time the line to Whitby was experiencing a rise in passenger numbers which required additional services, especially during the summer, nine trains in the Up direction from Saltburn but only eight corresponding trains in the Down direction from Scarborough. In 1933 the northern originating station for these trains changed from Saltburn to Middlesbrough and this remained the case until services on the Saltburn to Brotton section of the coast-line ended in September 1957.

The original station masters house at North Skelton survived intact as a private dwelling for many years until it was the target of arson attacks. The first occurred on April 11th, 2017, and a second on the 24th of September 2018 leaving it a derelict shell. Its original, mostly wooden, construction made it susceptible to such attacks. The photo (below) taken on the 22nd of May 2019 shows the parlous condition it was in. Total demolition occurred after a controlled burn on the 31st of August 2019.

Figures published about 1910 gave the number of tickets issued at North Skelton as 24,079. For comparison, the numbers at Brotton were not a lot different at 27,746, whereas Boosbeck issued over twice as many at 50,304 and Saltburn a whopping 144,236! However, when we compare the amount of ironstone credited to the stations only two have figures quoted, Brotton at 89,730 tons and North Skelton with 323,101, evidence if needed of the importance of ironstone mining to the area. After the growth of bus services during the 1920's and 30's, passenger numbers at all the stations in East Cleveland fell markedly. It would have come as no surprise that lightly used stations, like North Skelton, would have closed so early in British Railways days, it being one of a number of pre-Beeching closures. Known Station Masters at North Skelton are shown below.

Information from Pension Records held in the Ken Hoole Centre Darlington Railway Museum

Name	Initials	Date	From	To
CHARLTON?		1902		
CHARLTON	W. H.	-/07/1914	NORTH SKELTON	LOFTUS
WHITELOCK	J.	-/10/1914	MONK FRYSTON	NORTH SKELTON
WHITELOCK	F.	-/02/1921	NORTH SKELTON	WORMALD GREEN
COULL	S. H.	-/04/1921	FERRYBRIDGE	NORTH SKELTON
COULL?		-/03/1935		
STABLER	A.	-/03/1935	SHILDON	NORTH SKELTON
STABLER	R.	-/11/1935	NORTH SKELTON	HUNWICK
ELLERTON	R.	-/03/1936	ROMALDKIRK	NORTH SKELTON
ELLERTON	R.	-/06/1937	NORTH SKELTON	CLIFTON MOOR
CAIL	N. R.	-/06/1937	CRAMLINGTON	NORTH SKELTON
CAIL	N. R.	-/05/1941	NORTH SKELTON	SWALWELL
SMITH	W.	-/07/1941	BARTON HILL	NORTH SKELTON
SMITH	W.	-/01/1949	NORTH SKELTON	RAVENSTONEDALE
NOBLE	G. H.	-/05/1949	BROTTON	NORTH SKELTON
NOBLE	G. H.	-/06/1952	NORTH SKELTON	WILLINGTON

To balance ironstone exported from the area, a corresponding flow of incoming goods traffic was required to further increase the profitability of the local railways. Foremost amongst these was coal from County Durham. The scale of this trade can be gauged by the number of domestic coal depots that once existed in the area: Longacres (Skelton), Slapewath, Boosbeck, Priestcroft, Stanghow, Wilkinson's siding, Lumpsey, Brotton, Saltburn, Redcar, Marske and possibly North Skelton. Also there was a depot at Kilton Thorpe. Coal & coke was also needed for the Steelworks at Skinningrove and to feed the boilers at the pits in the area. Coal for domestic use was unloaded by hand from open wagons or via purpose built coal drops where the coal was unloaded by gravity from an elevated stage into individual 'cells' that provided the merchant with a means of separating different types of fuel. Both methods survived well into the 20th century as shown by the photographs below.

Previous page (top) is 16-ton coal wagon B579836 at Carlin How 3rd of January 1984 and (below) 21-ton coal wagon B429718 at Brotton the same day. When this service was withdrawn, in 1984, only three depots survived: Saltburn, Brotton and Carlin How. A local resident Edna Owens (nee Dowson) remembers going with her father to collect coal from North Skelton station in a cart or wheelbarrow, providing evidence that household coal traffic from there took place. Such trade was a perk of the station master's job and it could be quite lucrative. The coming of the railways would have greatly reduced the cost of fuel for the average household, meaning that they might have had more money available to spend on a few little luxuries, like a day trip to the seaside. Further revenue for the area's railways came from the transportation of more general goods. Indeed, prior to the arrival of motor transport after the Great War, the railways carried out the role of General Carriers; just about anything could be, and was, carried by them. To cater for this trade, large Goods sheds were erected at North Skelton, Boosbeck, Brotton and Saltburn.

Longacres Mine & Coal Depot

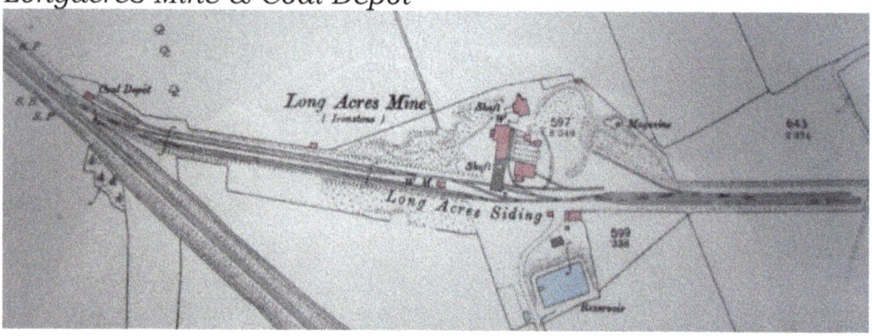

Crown Copyright 1893 Ordnance Survey (Published 1894)

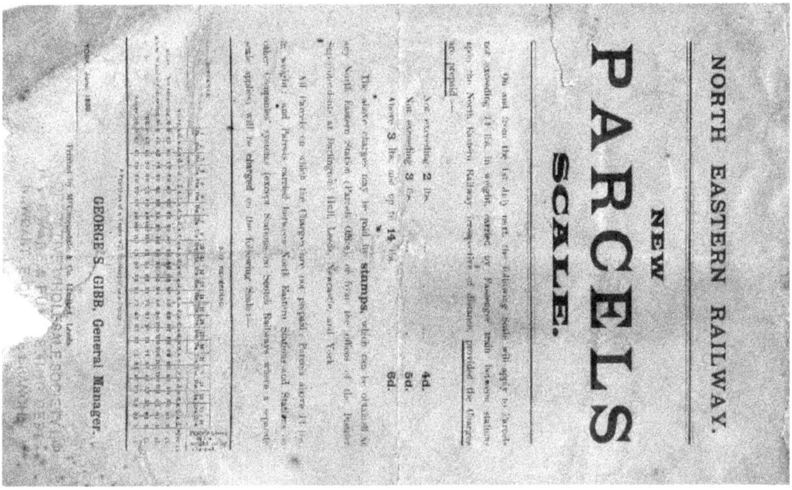

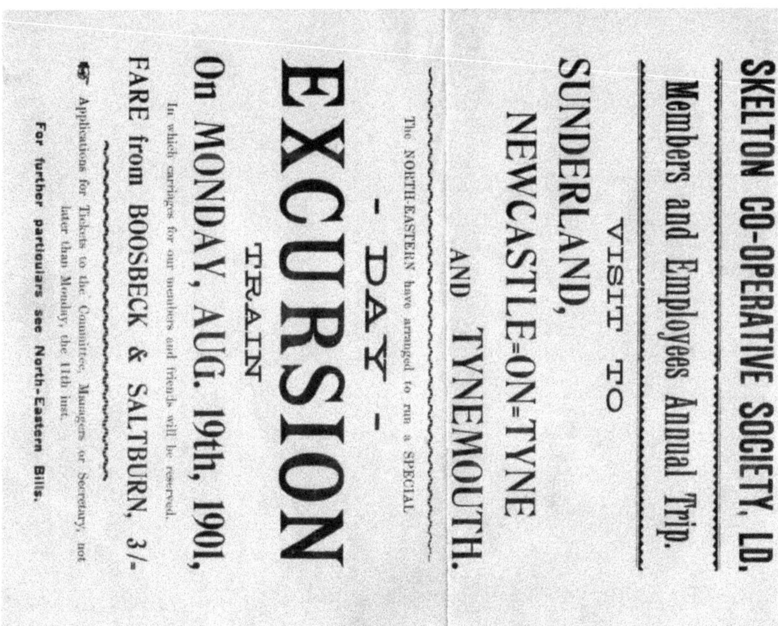

(Top) Parcels notice 1898, 4 years before opening
(Bottom) Excursion notice1901, the year before opening

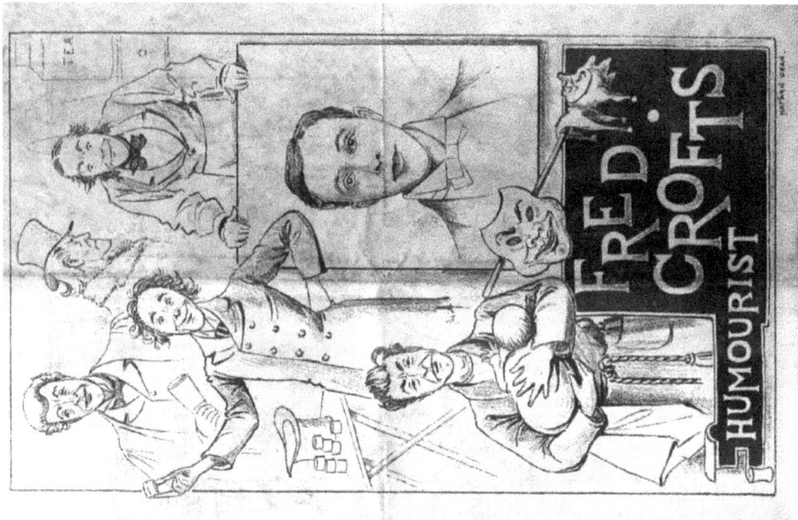

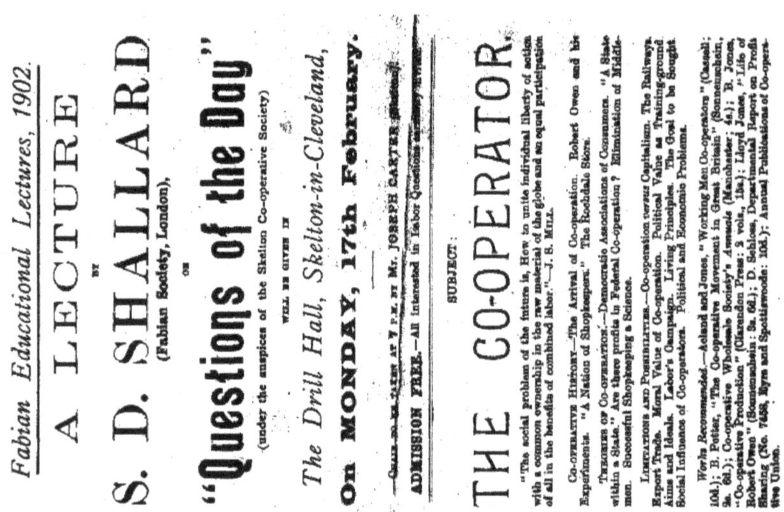

Fabian Educational Lectures, 1902.

A LECTURE

BY

S. D. SHALLARD

(Fabian Society, London),

ON

"Questions of the Day"

(under the auspices of the Skelton Co-operative Society)

WILL BE GIVEN IN

The Drill Hall, Skelton-in-Cleveland,

On MONDAY, 17th February.

CHAIR TO BE TAKEN AT 7 P.M. BY MR. JOSEPH CARTER

ADMISSION FREE.—All interested in Labor Questions

SUBJECT:

THE CO-OPERATOR.

"The social problem of the future is, How to unite individual liberty of action with a common ownership in the raw material of the globe and an equal participation of all in the benefits of combined labor."—J. S. MILL.

CO-OPERATIVE HISTORY.—The Arrival of Co-operation. Robert Owen and his Experiments. "A Nation of Shopkeepers." The Rochdale Store.

THEORIES OF CO-OPERATION.—Democratic Associations of Consumers. "A State within a State." Are there profits in Federal Co-operation? Elimination of Middlemen. Successful Shopkeeping a Science.

LIMITATIONS AND POSSIBILITIES.—Co-operation *versus* Capitalism. The Railways. Export Trade. Moral Value of Co-operation. Political Value as Training-ground. Aims and Ideals. Labor's Campaign. Living Principles. The Goal to be Sought. Social Influence of Co-operators. Political and Economic Problems.

Works Recommended.—Acland and Jones, "Working Men Co-operators" (Cassell; 10d.); B. Potter, "The Co-operative Movement in Great Britain" (Sonnenschein, 2s. 6d.); Co-operative Wholesale Society's *Annuals* (Manchester; 4s.); B. Jones, "Co-operative Production" (Clarendon Press: 2 vols., 15s.); Lloyd Jones, "Life of Robert Owen" (Sonnenschein: 3s. 6d.); D. Schloss, Departmental Report on Profit Sharing (No. 7458, Eyre and Spottiswoode: 10d.); Annual Publications of Co-operative Union.

The posters (from the author's collection) demonstrate how things changed in Skelton and East Cleveland even before North Skelton Station opened. If we return to the cost of the stagecoach quoted at the start of this work where the lowest cost was some 5d per mile it can be seen how railways had reduced the cost of travel and placed it within the grasp of a greater proportion of the population. For a 3/- fare, people could travel for example between Boosbeck and Sunderland, about 55 miles by rail at just over ½d per mile, a considerable reduction even allowing for inflation. Fred Crofts the Humourist, what we would call today a comedian or impressionist, came from the Manchester area, a journey before the railway age that would have been difficult and long. The Railways also helped people from areas of high unemployment, for example Cornwall and East Anglia, to come to find a job in the mines and steel works that proliferated at this time.

Finally, we need to look at how the Railways in Skelton and East Cleveland declined even before the infamous cuts of Dr Beeching, a process that was long and painful. First to go was the mineral branch to Stanghow (Margrove Park) pit in 1926, followed by the Skelton Park branch in 1939, just prior to the 2nd world war. Next was our station, North Skelton, closing initially on the 15th of January 1951 as a result of the Government directing British Railways to reduce its weekly coal consumption by 10,000 tons so that the National Coal Board could export high grade steaming coal to earn foreign capital. It did however reopen on the 18th of June for the summer timetable, only for final closure to occur on the 10th of September 1951. Goods services lasted until the 1st of February 1952 when they, too, were withdrawn only to be reinstated in October 1956 when it reopened as a private siding, presumably for the importation of materials for North Skelton Mine. Coincidentally when this mine closed on January 17th, 1964 the goods service at North Skelton was also withdrawn from the 21st of that month. The final trainload of Cleveland iron ore, some 200 tons, had been despatched on the 20th of January.

The Loftus to Whitby section of the coastal line closed to all traffic on 3rd of May 1958. After a brief respite passenger services from Loftus, Brotton & Boosbeck were withdrawn on

30th of April 1960 when the Brotton to Guisborough section closed to all traffic excepting Boosbeck as noted below. The final passenger service from Guisborough to Middlesbrough ended on 2nd of March 1964. Some goods services lingered a little longer; the Lingdale and Kilton branches went in 1962 and 1963 respectively, which left only the short branch to North Skelton which, as mentioned above, went in 1964. Goods services were withdrawn from Boosbeck (fed from Brotton) on 12th of September 1964 and Guisborough on the 31st of August 1964. From that point on, we were left with our nearest passenger station being at Saltburn, exactly as it had been in 1865!

Happily, the 1872 Saltburn Extension line is still with us today and passes the site of North Skelton station. The line was singled in 1970 when steelmaking ceased at Skinningrove works and sees daily steel trains from Skinningrove and Potash, Salt & Polyhalite from Boulby Mine (on a section of the former coastal line re-laid in 1972). In the 1980's it was hoped to reintroduce a passenger service as in the intervening years the population of the area had greatly increased, however Central Government were not very supportive about the idea, choosing to spend the available funds in other parts of the country. But as our Victorian forbearers have proved you need to be determined to prevail. Who knows, perhaps in the future, Skelton will once again have its own station.

To conclude, preserved steam engine LNER K1 2-6-0 number 62005 is seen passing the site of the former North Skelton station. The station master's house can be seen at the right-hand side, still intact on 10th of May 2008. The K1 locomotive is in almost the same place as the earlier photograph of the A8 in the 1950's.

References

Mike Hitches *'Steam Around Middlesbrough'* Amberley Publishing 2014

G.W.J Potter *'A History of the Whitby & Pickering Railway'* S.R. Publishers Limited 1969 (2nd Ed)

William Weaver Tomlinson *'North Eastern Railway'* David & Charles 1967

Peter Tuffs *'Cleveland Gazetteer of Ironstone Mines'* Peter Tuffs 1996

Geoffrey Allen Collection – Photographs & Documents

Ken Hoole Centre, Darlington Railway Museum

North Skelton Station photographs

Pension Records

History of Skelton for the year1881 (Web Site)

Home Words for Heart & Hearth, Skelton Magazine 1895 & 1898

Home Words for Heart & Hearth, Skelton & Boosbeck Magazine 1902

British Rail Track Diagrams 2 Eastern & Anglia Regions – Quail Map Company 1996 (Reprint)

Colin Berwick - www.nymcam.co.uk/kcy31b.htm

Letters page, Steam World Issue 386, August 2019 Steam World Publishing (closure of North Skelton)

Auto Train in Guisborough Station – Evening Gazette Live

Ordnance Survey Map of 1894 (Crown Copyright) Longacres Coal Depot

Social change in Skelton 1872-1914

Josie Bland

Skelton residents are proud of the community spirit which exists in the village. It was the guiding light behind the many Heritage projects described in this booklet. This article demonstrates how the community was formed. It attempts to explain how the uncontrolled mass of young workers who arrived in droves in the mid-19th century to man the new ironstone industry, were gradually tamed to form a close-knit and stable society.

Shortly after the first Gala Day of the Cleveland Miners' Association was held at Skelton (May 1st, 1872) a letter was printed in *The Daily Gazette,* setting out the ideal to which working men should aspire.

> *...be sober men, be industrious men, be moral men: look to the comfort and happiness of your families and your own comfort and happiness will most naturally follow...look to the education of your children; see that they go regularly to school and see that they improve their minds with useful knowledge during the week, then send them to school on Sunday afternoon so they may have an opportunity of a moral and religious education.*

George Spink Daily Gazette 22 May 1872

This chapter will examine how the mining community of Skelton moved nearer to this ideal, with the help of organisations aimed at radically improving the lives of the working class.

If we rewind to the middle of the 19th century, we witness the discovery of deep ironstone seams in the Cleveland Hills, at Skinningrove in 1847 and Eston in 1850. Extracting the ore was labour intensive. A large work force was needed; miners and would-be miners from declining industries all over Britain arrived to man this new enterprise. They came in their thousands; tin and copper miners from Cornwall, coal miners from Scotland, Wales, Durham and the West Riding, and agricultural labourers from Lincolnshire and East Anglia. A population explosion was the inevitable result. The small village of Skelton changed dramatically. It had played a part in the earlier alum industry, but ironstone mining was on a different scale altogether. Around its core of tradespeople and farmers, the village rapidly expanded. Heavy industry came to its doorstep. Longacre, Park Pit and North Skelton mines were sunk and started producing between 1870 and 1875. The Saltburn Extension Branch of the North Eastern Railway opened in 1878 carrying the excavated iron ore to the Middlesbrough iron works, and rows of new houses were hastily thrown up.

Skelton in the 1850s and 1860s was a melting pot, more like the American Frontier than Merrie England, dominated by testosterone-driven, wild, young men seeking work. In the early years of the East Cleveland mining industry its profits offered little benefit to the work force. Life was brutal, with poor working conditions, numerous appalling accidents, and job security virtually nil. The mine owners would hire and fire according to the market demand for iron ore. Living conditions were basic, houses badly built, dirty and unhygienic. In 1880 four streets in nearby Boosbeck actually collapsed – the mining tunnels that ran beneath them were not sufficiently shored up.

It's likely that, at first, these incomers couldn't understand each other. When you first mix Scottish, Welsh and Geordie accents with numerous other dialects, then add in local languages such as the Cornish spoken by the tin and copper miners, it is inevitable that communication will be a problem. Isolated, and experiencing dreadful working and living conditions it is not surprising that the young, male workforce was violent, usually drunk, and given to petty crime and poaching. Change had to happen. Somehow this ragbag of disparate individuals from all corners of Britain needed to cohere and become a community.

Change came slowly. A series of Mining Acts slowly regulated working conditions and Education Acts ensured literacy amongst the mining community. Allotments of land were given to provide a leisure activity away from the pub and enable fresh food to be put on the table. And change also came in the form of organisations that were set up for the working class, some by the working class, others by members of the middle and upper classes aimed at working class improvement. Trade Unions, Chapels of various denominations, the Co-operative Society, Libraries, Reading Rooms, the provision of Allotments and the Temperance Movement all played a part in civilising the Wild West that was Skelton, turning many wild, drunk, single youths into hard-working, sober and responsible family men.

It was no coincidence that many of the trade union leaders in this area were also lay preachers and Temperance society members. They were the role models for the workers of Skelton.

'Be Industrious men'

NORTH YORKSHIRE AND CLEVELAND MINERS AND QUARRYMEN'S ASSOCIATION

Trade Unions were of major importance in improving the lot of the working man. Previously banned, in 1871 they were legalised by Gladstone's Liberal government. By 1872 a firebrand of a miner called Joseph Shepherd had brought together miners from the length and breadth of East Cleveland to form the North Yorkshire and Cleveland Ironstone Miners' Association (the CMA). The three new mines were reaching completion, and the price of iron ore was high. It was a good time to ask for improvements to working conditions and pay. The first meeting of the CMA took place on May 1st, 1872, and it was estimated that over 7000 miners attended, with Alexander MacDonald, the leader of the National Mineworkers Association, the main speaker. These meetings, that occurred once or twice a year, were known as Gala or Demonstration Days, and were, more often than not, held in Skelton on Hollybush Farm's land (now part of the Industrial Estate). Miners came from all over East Cleveland and beyond with the CMA's membership stretching from Eston and Normanby to Rosedale. For many miners and their wives, the Gala days offered amusements, food and fun. Each village had its band, and the miners marched behind it to the field on Hollybush Farm carrying their large trade union banners.

Brotton branch of the CMA on a Gala Day.

Some will have heard the earnest speeches from the Trade Unionists who were up on the hay wagon that acted as a platform, but many will have treated the day as a holiday. If they *had* listened on that first day, they would have heard Alexander MacDonald demanding fewer hours, better pay and better working conditions, and the right to an education for all. As the writer of the Gazette letter stated: *'look to the education of your children'.*

Hard- drinking Joseph Shepherd was asked to step down from his role as Secretary to the CMA in 1876 due to his drunkenness, and some doubts about his bookkeeping. Contrast him with Joseph Toyn who was made President in 1875 and remained at the helm until 1911. Toyn was a powerful role model, a perfect example of the ideal family man, the antithesis of Shepherd. The illegitimate son of a Lincolnshire agricultural labourer, he was self-educated and, as well as leading the CMA, he became the President of the Skelton Co-operative Society, a lay preacher in the Methodist Chapel, and a local magistrate. Although self-taught, he demonstrated sophisticated skills in diplomacy, so much so that the Cleveland Miners avoided major strikes during his long period in office. Nevertheless, Toyn was no pushover and fought long and hard for worker's rights. Slowly, conditions did improve although the job was always arduous and dangerous, and work was not always guaranteed due to slumps in trade.

'Look to the comfort and happiness of your families'
THE SKELTON CO-OPERATIVE SOCIETY

For Skelton mining families every penny counted, so the opening of a shop that paid them back part of their shopping bill was eagerly awaited. Initially, it was the miners themselves, led by Joseph Toyn, who opened and ran the Skelton branch of the Co-operative Society, which first opened in 1873 at 73 High Street, formerly a shoe and boot shop, now the Skelton Pantry.

The Co-operative movement had been growing in size since its appearance in Rochdale in the 1840s. Its aim was to provide good quality food and hardware to the working population; a necessity because the unregulated buying and selling of commodities had resulted in corrupt trade practices. Overcharging, and the sale of poor-quality food, usually adulterated, were ongoing problems. Sell-by dates and the Trade Descriptions Act were the stuff of fantasy in the 19th century. The Co-op began buying in bulk from trusted sources with the intention of providing goods of consistent quality and, in tandem, set up its own manufacturing outlets. This led to the Co-op's overall name change, in 1863, to the Co-operative Wholesale Society, or CWS.

Staff in front of Co-op store, Skelton High Street 1905

The Co-op's philosophy differentiated it from other retail organisations. Of paramount importance was the fact that the Co-op was, and still is, non- profit making, stating that profit should be returned to the customer as Dividend. The customer became, in effect, a shareholder; the men and women who shopped at the Co-op also owned it. In Skelton in the late 1800s the Dividend was a staggering 20%. The first management committee of the Skelton Cooperative Society was made up of miners, with Joseph Toyn as chairman. And in the early years at Skelton, the same miners, including Toyn, served behind the counter, women being confined to the back rooms, although subsequent photographs of the Co-op staff show that women soon moved to the front counters of the store.

Within two years the Skelton Co-op had proved so successful that it needed to expand and in September 1875 it moved to its present premises. A meeting was held there a few weeks before its opening and a newspaper report states that it had 'front shop, store and showroom, a committee room, a reading room and a house for the storekeeper'. It provided a range of services, including a savings scheme with the Skelton Provident Society, and offered mortgages to allow the working man to own his own home. This was seen as important. Usually mine owners owned the miners' cottages and there was always the threat of eviction due to lack of work, strike action, old age, or illness.

The speech made at that August meeting in Skelton by the head of the Middlesbrough Co-operative was biblical. He stated that *"Some joined (the Co-op) to benefit themselves alone but a true co-operator would not be content with that. He would feel the spirit of The Great Teacher of Nazareth, the spirit of Love to his neighbour. Co-operation would lift him out of the trammels of poverty to the platforms of liberty"*. Co-operation, he claimed *"aimed at an improved condition of the working man; a state by which he could leave his mark behind him, and when he left this world , others would say of him 'He did well in his time and his memory is dear'"*. This speaker wanted working men *"to gain more intelligence ... and cling to cooperation as to a rock to save themselves from the engine of starvation, leaving the world in a better state than they found it"*. Religious belief and a belief in education, hence the reading room in the Co-op and the speech at the pre-opening party, were central to the Co-op's philosophy. Its own magazine, *The Wheatsheaf* was wordy and deeply serious.

Numerous Skelton families still have their Dividend books and can remember their own, or their mother's 'Divvi' number. The little bank, where the Dividend was handed out, still exists, a reminder of the days when the miners and their families lived hand to mouth and the Dividend pay-out often was a life-saver. In old Dividend books we see the lists of weekly shopping and they make visible the budgets of the miners' wives and the care and attention they gave to feeding and clothing their families. Obtaining mortgages, taking out an insurance policy and writing a weekly shopping list was something that previous mining generations would have found impossible. The big difference in 1875, when Skelton's present Co-op opened, was the fact that more people were learning to read.

'Look to the education of your children'
EDUCATION, LITERACY, THE LENDING LIBRARY AND THE LITERARY INSTITUTE

Until 1870, on the marriage certificates of the Skelton miners and others from the labouring class, it's likely that the bride and groom's signatures would only consist of a cross. After 1870, we increasingly see the cross replaced by a written signature demonstrating that the bride and groom could read and write. It was the Education Act of 1870 and subsequent Acts of Parliament that enabled this, giving all children access to Elementary education.

Before 1870 all schools charged fees. The wealthy had their Public (boarding) Schools, tutors and governesses, whilst the more affluent parents in towns and villages such as Skelton paid for their children to go to small village day schools. In 1831, Skelton, with a population of 781 had five day schools containing 52 boys and 70 girls, but the poor had little or no access to these. In 1856 John Thomas Wharton paid for the building of a school, which became one of the local primary schools when compulsory education was introduced.

We get a glimpse of mid-century Victorian education from the pages of Dickens. Gradgrind's establishment in *Hard Times*, where facts were paramount and little else was taught was based on village schools, whilst the worst excesses of the boarding system are illustrated by the dreadful Whackford Squeers and his school, Dotheboys Hall, in *Nicholas Nickleby*.

In 1870 the Liberal government introduced Board Schools. These were non-denominational elementary schools run by School Boards, their members voted in by the local ratepayers.

Initially, parents had to pay a small fee, not more than 9d but this was scrapped in 1879. In 1880 elementary education became compulsory, although there was much truancy due to older children being needed to help in the home or bring home wages. However, as the younger children began school at the age of three, schools provided a much-needed breathing space from child care for mothers with large families. The two Board Schools in Skelton Village itself were on Stanghow Lane, and on Cross Green. Children were taught reading, writing and arithmetic, and did a lot of copying.

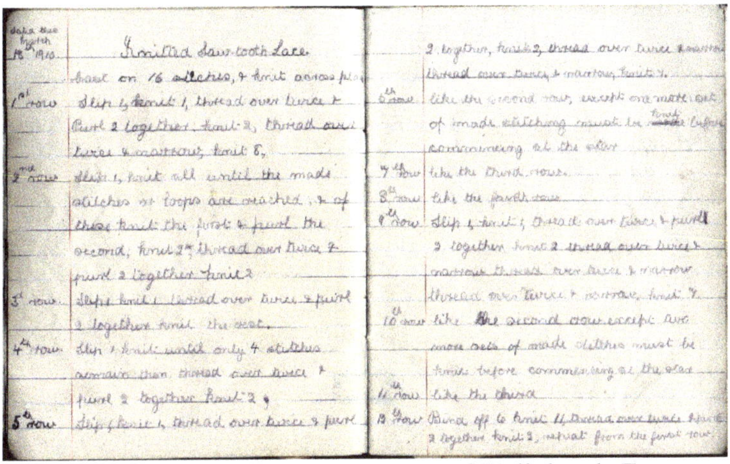

Knitted Saw-tooth Lace.

Cast on 16 stitches, & knit across plain

1st row Slip 1, knit 1, thread over twice & purl 2 together, knit 2, thread over twice & narrow, knit 8,

2nd row Slip 1, knit all until the made stitches or loops are reached, & of these knit the first & purl the second; knit 2, thread over twice & purl 2 together knit 2

3rd row Slip 1 knit 1 thread over twice & purl 2 together knit the rest.

4th row Slip 1 knit until only 4 stitches remain then thread over twice & purl 2 together knit 2,

5th row Slip 1 knit 1, thread over twice & purl 2 together, knit 2, thread over twice & narrow thread over twice & narrow, knit 4.

6th row like the second row, except one more set of made stitches must be knit before commencing at the star

7th row like the third rows.

8th row like the fourth row

9th row Slip 1 knit 1, thread over twice & purl 2 together knit 2 thread over twice & narrow thread over twice & narrow thread over twice & narrow, knit 2.

10th row like the second row except two more sets of made stitches must be knit before commencing at the star

11th row like the third

12th row Bind off 6 knit 1, thread over twice & purl 2 together knit 2, repeat from the first row.

Schoolbook of Alice Emmerson of Hollybush Farm
On these pages, Alice has copied a knitting pattern. In later life, she became landlady of The Royal George.

It appears religious practice was kept to a minimum, presumably because of the differing beliefs of church and chapel. In 1896 the local School Board instructed schoolteachers to only use the Lord's Prayer and to read passages from the Bible without comment.

The government's decision to make schooling compulsory was based on industry's need for a literate work force, one that could read and do simple arithmetic. Truancy apart, it seems that by the turn of the century, the majority *could* read, but by then the battle over what they *should* read was well under way. There was a chasm between what the labouring class wanted to read, and what the middle and upper classes thought they ought to read. The *News of the World* was first published on October 1st, 1843 so, by the time the village underwent its population explosion this type of newspaper, with its fake news and spurious gossip, was well established. Book publishers too, aiming more at a female audience, produced cheaply printed, simplistic and dramatic novellas known as *Penny Dreadfuls.* Whilst the 3^{d} charge for the *News of the World* and the buying of books were out of the reach of most mining families presumably this obstacle was overcome by sharing one copy amongst many.

A typical *'Penny Dreadful'*

The drive to establish a library in Skelton and to open a literary institute was in part a reaction against the excesses of the popular press but was also fuelled by a genuine desire to improve the lot of the workers by giving them access to 'decent' reading material and a quiet place to read it. This philanthropic cause was backed by fund raising concerts and the setting up of committees.

In 1875 the Co-op's newly opened premises at their present location in Skelton High Street included a reading room. The Secretary of the Cleveland Miners' Association and Chairman of the Skelton Co-operative Society, Joseph Toyn, had taught himself to read believing that literacy was the first step to self-betterment.

On 28th October 1876, the Skelton Literary Club met for the first time. It was a meeting place for those in Skelton who could read and enjoyed reading, to discuss literature and to read aloud. The local *Gazette* described it as follows: *"The club is the only attempt to supply reading, recreation and instruction during the winter months as there is neither library, news room or anything of that kind in the village"*. The Literary Club set about putting this right and on 10th March 1880 it held a fund-raising concert for the hoped-for Skelton Library. They claimed to already own 400 good quality books. In 1882, having grown their collection, they decided to lend their books free to the public. Many more concerts followed and finally the library opened in tandem with the new Literary Institute, on 4th November 1901. This was a recreational facility paid for (£2,000) by the Wharton Family and contained a billiards room, reading room, the library, lecture room and two committee rooms. It was intended for all – including the poor – and the committee was made up from a social and political mix of members.

It did not take long for the *Gazette* to report that the billiard room was used far more than the library. The 'Lit' and the library were examples of one class determining what was suitable for the recreation of another. One committee member could not understand why the public didn't take the 'quality' books to read, especially as some were about the mining industry.

Although the 'Lit' was demolished in 1993, the library continues to function as a social space, very much as its predecessor did over a hundred years ago. As well as lending books, it is a quiet space to read the newspapers, to hold group meetings, to meet the local councillors, and to engender community spirit.

But back in the 19th century, as well as developing their literacy with the help of improving books or more likely the *News of the World*, the miners also needed fresh air and exercise and allotments provided the perfect solution.

'Be industrious men – look to the comfort and happiness of your families'

ALLOTMENTS

What better way to be both industrious and to look to the comfort of the family than by working an allotment of land. The miner would be out in the open, get fresh air and exercise, and would provide food for his wife and children. And, of course, it would keep him out of the pub! Allotments were commonplace in the late nineteenth century, and did indeed supplement wages with fresh food, home grown vegetables, eggs and possibly meat in the form of chickens or even a slaughtered pig.

The provision of allotments has a chequered history. Over the centuries, landowners enclosed more and more of their land, including the common land around their manors, where the poor had grown a few vegetables and kept some hens. 'Commoners' were compensated by allotments of land attached to tied cottages. Gradually this right was eroded until the 1801 Enclosure Act led to every scrap of 'free' land being claimed for landowners who were developing techniques that allowed them to produce crops more efficiently. Added to this were draconian punishments for poaching, for example the large man traps triggered by pressure plates, the teeth of which could take off a man's leg. But by 1845, the wealthy and powerful did an about turn as there was a real fear that the people's uprisings happening elsewhere in Europe could spread to Britain. The government at the time required that if land was enclosed, a percentage had to be set aside for allotment use. The 1887 Allotment Act made this request law, demanding that parish councils provide allotments. This Act was reinforced in 1907 by the Smallholding and Allotments act.

A smallholding on the High Street

Allotment workers, John Street, New Skelton.

Residents of Skelton without land were offered allotments from the Parish council in much the same venues as now, but added to this the Wharton Estate, the administrative arm of the Castle, provided allotments to those who rented cottages from them. These could be used as a bargaining tool. In 1879 a public footpath from North Skelton to Saltburn was fenced off by the estate bailiff, Mr Hamilton, probably to deter poachers, as part of it crossed estate land. Miss Hannah Emmerson, who lived on a farm near to the path and who used the path regularly, asked one of her farm hands to pull the fence down. She was threatened with court proceedings and the miners rallied round her, planning a demonstration walk along the route. The estate bailiff came to one of their meetings threatening to take their 'gardens' (allotments) away from them if they continued with this action. The miners did continue. On the 6th January 1880, over 800 miners and Skelton residents walked from North Skelton to Saltburn. The estate backed down, and the footpath that the protestors walked along remains open to this day.

The romantic notion of the ruddy faced miner, digging with gusto and bringing armfuls of food home for his adoring wife and chubby children is perhaps a view that the middle and upper classes wished for, a manifestation of their desire to control the lower orders. But just as no amount of library provision could stop the public reading *Penny Dreadful*s and the *News of the World* newspaper, so providing allotments did not automatically lead to rational, healthy outdoor recreation. The council could not prevent the home brewing, the cock fighting and dog fighting, and the many other subversive activities that took place behind the potting sheds.

The mention of home brewing leads to the next section of this chapter, showing how the great social evil of drunkenness was tackled in Skelton, and, by implication, throughout Victorian Britain.

'Be sober men'
TEMPERANCE

Whilst reading rooms, libraries and allotments were being provided, and the Co-op offered unadulterated food and a dividend for buying it, the improvements in the workers' lives were easily undermined by the demon drink: beer!

During the 18th century, anti-drink campaigns had been directed at spirits, particularly gin. Beer was represented at this time as a symbol of Britishness - and healthy. Drinking water, particularly in crowded urban areas was often contaminated, thus beer seemed a safer alternative. But during the 19th century, as industrialisation gained a stranglehold on Britain, the realisation came that the problems associated with spirits were equalled by those caused by beer. It was quite common in the early 19th century for workmen to get their pay in the alehouse, often the paymasters arrived late by which time the men had already spent most of their wages. In a home with little money, in a family that was struggling to survive, lack of their husband/father's wages was catastrophic. Working class drunkenness was also all far too visible, workers choosing the warmth of the public house, to the cold and squalor of their homes. Drunken, often violent behaviour was a major cause for concern in the East Cleveland villages, and magistrates seemed to be dealing with inebriated miscreants to the exclusion of all else.

The drink problem was the impetus behind the Temperance and Teetotal Movements, both emerging in the early decades of the 19th century. The first promoted drinking in moderation, but preferably not at all, the second was more hard-line, requiring total abstinence from alcohol. The Temperance movement, begun in the 1820s, contained a diverse range of individuals: industrialists, especially Quakers, who wanted to constrain the drinking habits of their workmen, and political radicals who saw a drop in drink revenue as weakening the government's pocket. The Teetotal movement first saw light of day at the time of the 1833 Beer Act, which allowed anyone to sell beer on purchase of a licence, at a fee of two guineas. A rapid rise in licensed premises was the result; although this was probably more to do with numerous, previously illicit, premises now selling beer legitimately. There may have been no more alehouses than existed before the bill.

Whilst the Temperance movement was *for* the working class, the Teetotal movement was formed *by* the working class, especially from an emerging faction of this class. This sector consisted of those who, like George Spink, the writer of the letter which opened this chapter, believed in self-improvement. They reasoned that through education, careful budgeting, a Christian outlook underpinned by regular attendance at chapel, and abstaining from drink, a man and his family could rise up the social ladder. We see the CMA President, Joseph Toyn, as a clear example of this type and we could include Co-op managers and aspirational staff.

As the ironstone industry hit Skelton, Temperance and Teetotalism emerged in tandem and appeared at their most potent in the last two decades of the 19th century. One of their earliest manifestations was the forming of a Band of Hope at Skelton. The Band of Hope was a teetotal movement, founded in Leeds in 1847 by Jabez Tunnicliff, a Baptist Minister. Its aim was to inform children about the dangers and evil of drink, so that they would be abstainers as adults. These children also had the onerous task of warning their parents about the problems associated with drunkenness.

Children as young as six were recruited, the meetings taking place in village halls, such as Skelton's Drill Hall, and chapel schoolrooms, there being a powerful link between methodism and teetotalism. Lectures on drink and other more cheerful topics were often given by 'magic lantern' an early form of what we now call a slide projector, and these meetings were supplemented by some form of excursion, perhaps to the seaside or the countryside. The old newspapers offer glimpses of The Band of Hope in Skelton. On January 7th 1888, the friends and members of the Band of Hope associated with the Parish Church met at the Drill Hall, Skelton for a magic lantern talk on local blast furnaces by Dr Stainthorpe of Kirkleatham which was *'largely attended'*. The *Gazette* pointed out that the talk was all the more interesting as the speaker had taken the pictures himself. Two months later, on the 3rd March the same group met, again in the Drill Hall, for a 'magic lantern' show of Scenes from the Continent. Seven hundred people packed the Drill Hall for another magic lantern show on February 14th 1890, although frustratingly we have no record of the subject, and on 6th April 1894 the Drill Hall was yet again the venue for a Band of Hope meeting with a Punch and Judy show paid for by Mrs Wharton of Skelton Castle. It might be argued that the children really came for events such as this and the excursions, nevertheless they were expected to sign a pledge that they would avoid alcohol throughout their lives.

Two Middlesbrough Potteries tea plates for the Temperance movement

The plate on the left has an illustration of children signing the pledge. That on the right has an illustration from George Cruikshank's series 'The Bottle'. Here, the drunkard's wife is having to pawn clothes and possessions to pay the drunken husband's debts.

As well as the Bands of Hope, Skelton was the home of several Temperance groups. Linked to church and chapel, they were active in the last decades of the 19th century particularly in the 1890s, and often had their own Temperance Bands.

Further back, in 1877 to be exact, the 14th meeting of the International Order of Good Templars (IOGT) Cleveland Lodge at Guisborough included representatives from Skelton. This group, which based their meetings and mode of dress on those of Freemasonry were highly active in East Cleveland. The organisation clearly had had a presence in this area since 1863. Thirty-three lodges (groups) and juvenile temples (children's groups) were represented and the chairman spoke of the growing zeal for temperance in the Cleveland area. The adult membership had reached nearly 2000 whilst the juvenile section had 1300 members. He claimed that many had joined with the idea of moderation in mind but had come to the conclusion that the only path was that of total abstinence. The members had vowed total abstinence from intoxication, tobacco, gambling and profanity. A children's competition with prizes was being organised. Questions would be asked on four books – *The Bible, The History and Mystery of a Glass of Ale, A Pint of Ale, What it Is and What it Costs,* and *Lecture on Malt.*

Eighteen years later, in 1895, the IOGT finally opened a lodge at Skelton. Named 'The Skelton Happy Home' it admitted 18 people at its first meeting. Already with a lodge at North Skelton, it had numerous other lodges in the East Cleveland area, including Boosbeck, Brotton, Carlin How, Guisborough, Margrove Park, Skinningrove, New Marske and Redcar.

In the 1881 census, we find that 14 North Terrace was a Temperance hotel, run by James Elliott, originally from Hutton Rudby. With the Royal George at 10 North Terrace and the Duke William at 16, this establishment provided an oasis of abstinence between two popular drinking venues. Its outward appearance would have echoed that of the regular public house, but its drinks were non-alcoholic. Examples of these would be Dandelion and Burdock, Cream Soda, Ginger Beer and the ever-popular Vimto. It was not on the 1871 or the 1891 census so how long it survived is unknown, but its presence is indicative of the groundswell of interest in the Temperance movement.

As the 20th century unfolded, the *Daily Gazette* reported on a visit, in July 1906, of Mr James Loysley, better known as 'The Battersea Navvy'. Mr Loysley visited the Parish and spoke on behalf of Church of England Temperance Society, giving open air lectures from the back of one of the Society's vans. The following extract from the *Daily Gazette* is a vivid account of Temperance activity. *"...On Monday the van was drawn through Skelton and found a good "pitch" between the Post Office and the Institute. On Tuesday it was at New Skelton; on Wednesday on the Green; on Thursday at North Skelton and on Friday back at the Institute. On Monday afternoon he addressed a meeting of Sunday school children on The Hills [where camp meetings are wont to be held]. His ready wit and racy style combined with full knowledge of his subject in all its bearings upon the lives of working men secured him an attentive hearing. He proved by facts and argument how temperance, religion and self-control raise and refine a man while self-indulgence, intemperance and sin degrade and ruin him. In the following week he visited Boosbeck, Lingdale and Margrove Park...*"

James Loysley's claim, that temperance and religion raise and refine a man, leads to the final example - a discussion of one of the key elements of social control, religion.

'Be moral men'
SKELTON'S CHURCH AND CHAPELS

Religious belief and practice were interwoven with all the organisations discussed in this article. They underpinned the ideas and beliefs of the Co-operative society and the Temperance movement, schools had Christianity embedded in their daily activity and had close links with the church and chapel, and several local trade unionists were also lay preachers.

The building of two new places of worship in Skelton, a Wesleyan chapel in 1877 and a new Anglican church in 1884, might suggest that religious practice was alive and well at this time, at the very least it shows the rapidly-growing population of the village. As already discussed in "Snapshot in Time", the different types of places of worship in the latter half of the 19th century echo the social structure of the village.

There had been a church in Skelton probably since Saxon times. The Boroughgate archaeological excavations, in 2018, found evidence of a village existing around the area of Back

Lane farm and, looking in a straight line from there to the Castle we find Old All Saints Church, a Georgian building on foundations that date back to the early 14th century. Medieval Boroughgate's function was to service Skelton Castle through its tradespeople and artisans and the church had the same function. Now largely unused, Old All Saints church was built in 1785-86 and its situation, next to the Castle, reflects its purpose. The layout of the church clearly shows the social order at the time. The three-tier pulpit is halfway down the church. Opposite is a small room, open to the church and containing a fireplace. Squire John Wharton and his successors would occupy this space, have a welcome fire lit in the winter, and have the vicar preach directly to them. Much of the money for the building of this place of worship came from the wealthier Skelton families, who bought a pew with a locking door, and had the family name painted on the wall at the end. Some of the names resonate down the centuries, old Skelton families like: Robinson, Dixon, Petch, Emmerson. They were prosperous farmers, skilled artisans, tradespeople, and so on. The nearer the pew was to the Squire's niche, the higher the owner's social standing in the village was likely to be.

Old All Saints Church
Looking towards the altar. Box pews are on either side and the three-tier pulpit can be seen on the right.

Old All Saints Church
View from the pulpit across to the Wharton family pew

Many of the pews faced the pulpit rather than the altar, including those in a second gallery (now removed) on the east wall of the nave. This demonstrates the importance of the sermon, which clearly had priority over the ceremony itself.

As Margaret Drazin points out in “Snapshot in Time”, much of the seating in the church was bought and owned, with few ‘free’ places. Thus it was no surprise that the labouring classes turned to dissenting forms of Christian worship, such as Methodism in it various forms. However, there was some fluidity in the class make up between these alternatives and the established church. Methodism was a religious sect founded by the charismatic preacher, John Wesley, aimed at the labouring classes and intended to make the gospel easier to understand. Its buildings – chapels rather than churches – were simpler in design than those of the Anglicans; the services contained much singing, and the texts were in English. The Primitive Methodists were a breakaway group who were evangelical and wished for even greater simplicity in their services. Their places of worship could be corrugated iron constructions or someone’s living room, examples being the chapels at North Skelton and Green Road, and the Mission Room at 8 Thomas Street.

A month after the first miners' gala in Skelton, in June 1872, mine owner David Dale gave a speech on the occasion of the laying of the foundation stone for the new Wesleyan chapel. Dale spoke of John Wesley the founder of Methodism, passing through Skelton on his preaching circuit, and he celebrated the fact that Methodism enjoyed increasing popularity. The new chapel was able to seat 600, a vast congregation by today's standards. The first Wesleyan chapel had been built in 1812, with the land for the building given by John Wharton, at that time the owner of Skelton Castle. This Squire had resisted pleas for land up till then, pointing out that Skelton already had a perfectly good church. However, Wharton had spent a considerable fortune on rebuilding the castle and needed funds for his candidacy as MP for Beverley. W Taylor, one of the local Methodist leaders, visited him. The elections were going to be held in York, and Taylor pointed out that some of the Methodist leaders, in their York headquarters, held considerable political influence. On hearing this, the Squire buried his objections and sold the land to the Methodists.

(left) Wesleyan Chapel, Skelton
(right) Primitive Methodist Chapel, North Skelton.

All Saints parish church 1884

So, now, the labouring classes had their own places of worship, and services were held in chapels of varying design, or in front rooms, as an alternative to the Anglican church that was All Saints. By the 1870s the old church that nestled at the end of Church Lane, near to the Castle, was deemed too small for the growing population and, in 1881, work began on a new Anglican church in the High Street to replace it, the tower being paid for by Squire JT Wharton, the then resident at Skelton Castle. The old medieval model, of a church by the castle to serve the castle, was replaced by a church in the heart of the community, on the High Street. All Saints was consecrated by the Archbishop of York and opened for business on October 14th, 1884. It could hold at least 700. It was highly regarded (if the national newspapers are to be believed) as a fine example of Neo–Gothic architecture. In 1887 newspapers nationwide commented on the ladies in the choir of the new church, who were dressed in surplices, just like their male counterparts. The *Manchester Evening News* pointed out that, although there were similar examples in London, Skelton was the only church in the north of England with surplice-clad lady choristers.

It appears that as the nineteenth century drew to a close, Skelton had a thriving church- and chapel-going community. But we must not assume all places in church and chapel were filled on Sundays. For many of the workforce, Sunday was a day for sleeping, literally the day of rest, and for others, drinking. But the church and chapel acted as a brake on the excesses of the latter and were a cohesive social force bringing the community together. Christian belief underpinned other organisations such as the Temperance movement and the Co-op, at least in its early days, and, as mentioned earlier, many trade union officials were also lay preachers. Then, as now, it had a huge influence on education, being embedded into classroom teaching and behind the morning assemblies. Both church and chapels ran Sunday Schools which fulfilled Spink's call. Temperance activities were conducted at both church and chapel.

CONCLUSION

The gradual coming together of a coherent community in Skelton happened over the latter half of the nineteenth century. The ironstone industry brought thousands to the area, mainly young men looking for work who were, at first, to live and labour in appalling conditions. This was reflected in their behaviour which was fuelled by drink. But as the century wore on, gradually, a more civilised society emerged, aided by a mixture of self-help: Trade Unions, Teetotalism, Primitive Methodism and the Co-operative Society, and help from above, be it central government with its Acts of Parliament, relating to Education, Allotments or Licensing, or local philanthropists who were to be found in most 'improving' activities such as the Temperance movement and the drive to furnish Skelton with a free library.

The Temperance movement is a distant memory, trade unions are a weakened force – but the Co-op still exists, and locals still dig their allotments, although from choice rather than necessity. The local primary school is flourishing and maintains its links with All Saints, and the library is very much at the heart of the village. Skelton-in-Cleveland today has a community that works together to achieve its goals and celebrate its heritage. Those of us who live in this village have much to be proud of.

'The Spirit of East Cleveland'
Sculpted by Bill Harling; erected 2019.

Acknowledgements

The Skelton Townscape Heritage project would not have been the success that it was without the hard work and dedication of many people. Their efforts, whether great or small, are acknowledged here. If any individuals or groups have been overlooked, it does not mean that your contribution wasn't appreciated, merely that there doesn't seem to be a record of it in the project files.

The Project Manager: John Haw

The Lead Applicants: Joyce White, Tony Harding and Pam Batts

Staff of Redcar & Cleveland Borough Council: Darren Edmends, Lawrence Kerrigan, Lydia Scarfe, Ian Stuart and Jane Turner, with particular thanks due to Jo Mead

Staff of Tees Valley Rural Action (Formerly Tees Valley Rural Community Council): Rita Lawson and Doff Pollard

The volunteers, from within the community, who served on the Partnership Board: Peter Appleton, Pam Batts, Mike Betterton, Bob Brunger, Jane Dauncey, Tony Harding, Jim Hartnett, Julia Hedges, Audrey Kirby, Angus McDonald, Gina McMahon, John Newman, Geoffrey Scott, Anthony Wharton, Joyce White , Stuart White, and Janice Wilson

The committee and members of Skelton Villages Civic Pride: Chair: Ian Johnson; Secretary: Pam Batts; Treasurer: Janice Wilson; Vice Chair: Majorie Matthews; Allan Batts, Sheila Brown, Gill Cowley, Stephanie Gabbitas, Brenda Harding, Julia Hedges, Anthea Johnson, Michael Matthews, Don Raspin, Wendy Raspin, Beryl Richardson, Joyce White and Stuart White

The Red Wyverns and Stockton Archers, without whom the medieval event would not have happened

The members of the following community groups: Bridgehill day service group, Skelton Library "Sharpen your mind", Skelton Library "Thursday Girls", Skelton Library users, Skelton Primary School, SVCP Coffee Morning attendees, Year 7 Art Students at Freebrough Academy (2017 & 2018)

Finally, individuals from the local communities and not previously mentioned, who participated in the various activities: Geoffrey Allen, Judith Arber, Kate Bartram, Geoff Bell, Josie Bland, Barbara Bonas, Elizabeth Bowes, Richard Bowes, Amy Brown, Lucy Brown, Stacey Campbell, Marion Carling, John Chapman, Megan Clamp, Geoff Clark, Maureen Clark, Steve Crown, David Dance, Paul Docherty, Margaret Drazin, Ursula Earl, Dave Errickson, Geoff Evans, Shelagh Evans, Janet Firmager, Gordon Ford, Kay Fothergill, Chelsea Greenwood, Nicola Greenwood, Brian Grierson, Helen Grierson, Liz Grove, Debbie Hadfield, Maureen Hall, Terence Hall, Merrion Haw, Derek Hedges, Arthur Hoggett, Beatrice Jackson, Diana Kelly, Helena Lowe, Tabatha Maud, Gina McMahon, Sara Mitchell, Bethany Morgan, Bryan Neale, Eugenie Noonan, Geraldine Nuttal, Steve Nuttal, Jennifer Ord, Jenny Parker, Linda Parker, Anne Peacock, Roger Pell, Thane Perry, Peter Price, Nick Raban-Williams, Alice Read, Gillian Read, Sue Richards, Fiona Riley, Kirsten Robinson, Helen Rowlands, John Rowlands, Kay Rush, Alan Simkins, Daphne Simmons, Jane Sinclair, David Souter , Trish Suffell, Lindsay Teasdale, Steve Walker, Denise Weighell-Newton, Ian Weighell-Newton, Howard Wilson, Ian Wilson

Lightning Source UK Ltd.
Milton Keynes UK
UKHW021034040521
383090UK00007B/72

9 780993 36743